D1350648

VERITAS

First published 2004 by
Veritas Publications
7/8 Lower Abbey Street
Dublin 1
Ireland
Email publications@veritas.ie
Website www.veritas.ie

ISBN 1 85390 840 1

Cover design by Mick O'Farrell
Printed in the Republic of Ireland by Criterion, Dublin

*Veritas books are printed on paper made from the wood pulp of managed
forests. For every tree felled, at least one tree is planted, thereby renewing
natural resources.*

To Myles O'Farrell, as a tribute from all of us who were privileged to know him, and to our children: Denis, Donal, Lizann, Gabriel, Monica, Ursula, Inez, Joseph and Michael.

In memory also of Carl Berkeley, friend and colleague, who died on 20 July 2004, while this book, which was first suggested by him, was being prepared for publication.
Ar dheis Dé go raibh a anam dilis – may his dear soul be at the right hand of God.

Contents

Foreword

This book was first suggested by Carl Berkeley and arose from our discussion and debates about the person-centred approach, and our differing interpretations about some of the ideas and terms in the theory. For health reasons, Carl had to withdraw from the project, so the responsibility for the contents is solely mine.

I am frustrated by what appears at times to be a 'kindly but dismissive' response from many other counsellors and psychotherapists when discussing the theory within which I work. However, this is not an attempt to justify the person-centred approach (because I do not believe it needs justification), but so many books that are written about PCA presuppose quite a large knowledge of the basic theory and practice. These may not be readily accessible to beginners, who seek an introduction to what PCA entails, from self-actualisation and the special client/counsellor relationship, to the core conditions and conditions of worth. The words may be familiar, but for many their precise meaning may be somewhat obscure. This, then, is an attempt to distil the basic concepts into simple words without losing the integrity of the theory.

I hope to explain what these terms and definitions mean to me, how I encompass them in my own life and work, and to illustrate how valuable the person-centred approach can be in all relationships. The book will aim to help students understand how important it is for them to value their own unique characteristics within their work as person-centred counsellors, and to help them accept the uncertainty within that counselling work. The whole approach is more a way of being than merely a method of counselling. I would also like to help potential clients get a better awareness of the relationship they hope to enter into if they decide to seek counselling.

Definitions of counselling are difficult to formulate, as it is an endeavour which is more intangible than tangible, and invariably loses some of its flavour and impact when reduced to words and phrases. However, I have included some descriptions and definitions in the Appendix. Rather than focusing divisively on the differences (if any) between counselling and psychotherapy, I have identified some of the factors they hold in common, so that I can discuss the 'talking therapies' without becoming involved in controversy. The question of whether there is a difference between counselling and psychotherapy, and if there is, what that difference is, is far outside the scope of this handbook. I would hope that the 'dogma-eat-dogma' era of competitiveness between counselling and psychology and all the variations on these is drawing to a close, and that a new focus on both the common factors and what actually *works* is becoming evident. Sufficient to say that, for me, there is no difference in the work we do as counsellors or psychotherapists. In my opinion, the differences lie in the *description* of the work, to some extent in the training required by the different associations, and perhaps also in some territorial rivalry for status!

I have included case histories which serve to illustrate in practical terms the ideas and theories outlined, and where there is even the slightest possibility of a client being identified, permission to include their material has been granted. The use of he or she, his or hers, has been decided either on what seems to fit with the material, or on how I visualise the person I am writing about. I have always been very conscious of the debt I owe to my supervisee students, for their willingness to be open and creative in our sessions, and while I have acknowledged some of their experience, so much has become part of my own 'folklore' that I am sure there is an even greater amount of material unacknowledged.

I have tried to distil an entire theoretical framework within a short book, without losing the integrity of that theory, so there will surely be some unevenness and 'joins' visible. There would be far more were it not for the eagle eye and careful reading of my editor, Helen Carr, who also sent messages of encouragement whenever I flagged! My thanks also to my family and friends, who never complained when 'work on the book' was presented as a reason for not being able to participate in some event or meeting, but who were unfailing in their encouragement and enthusiasm. In the writing of this book there has been some element of a need to acknowledge the central place the theories of Carl Rogers have played in my life, and a further wish to share with other the benefits I have derived from adopting his 'way of being'. I hope I have succeeded in this, at least in some small measure.

1

Person-Centred Counselling

'For the therapist to be fully present as an understanding, caring person is highly important in making this process possible, though the most crucial events take place in the feelings and experiencings of the client.'[1]

Carl Rogers (1902-1987) was a psychologist in America who pioneered a major new approach in psychotherapy which was revolutionary and controversial at the time. He challenged the received wisdom of his day of the therapist as 'expert', and his ideas and their application are accepted widely today. His theories continue to create controversy, with many professionals in psychology, counselling and psychotherapy acknowledging his influence on their way of thinking and working, and almost as many minimising his impact. 'Rogers himself, however, never claimed that he had established the absolute truth about anything' and remained committed to ongoing learning.[2]

Rogers was reared in a conservative religious family and when he became a psychologist he initially worked with children. He began writing about his new theories in the nineteen thirties and forties, based on scientific enquiry and recorded sessions of his work. He used the word 'client' rather than 'patient' to underline his movement away from a medical model which held that people who came for help were 'ill' and needed to be 'cured'. He based his client-centred way of working on the basic assumption that every person, and every living organism, has a built-in tendency to actualise, or fulfill its potential, and that this potential can be thwarted when the organism encounters adverse conditions. Perhaps most controversially, he insisted that it was the client who knows where it hurts and how to proceed towards healing, throwing into question the whole idea of therapist as expert. For Rogers, the relationship between client and counsellor was a meeting of persons of equal worth, and without a power imbalance. His 'revolutionary' belief was that the counsellor's work lay not in solving problems, but rather in facilitating individuals to grow and develop within a climate of safety and trust fostered by certain qualities in the counsellor.

The titles used to refer to his work can be confusing, but they represent changes in the application of this work rather than theoretical changes. To begin with, Rogers called his way of working *client-centred*, since he was convinced that it was the client who knows 'where it hurts' and who has within the resources to change. The counsellor's task is to assist the client rather than to advise or direct him and the focus is on the attitudes of the counsellor towards the client rather than on any particular techniques. *'Non-directive'* was also used as a way of describing this emphasis on not advising or guiding the client, but this term came to be linked with an inaccurate image of the counsellor as being passive or inactive. As the *'Rogerian'* approach began to be used more widely in other fields such as education, cross-cultural communication and international peace work, the word 'client' became too narrow in its description, and it became known as 'person-centred', resulting in person-centred counselling or therapy 'we are at all times in this highly concentrated way committed as persons to other persons who seek our help.'[3] The term *person-centred approach* is used in the wider context to encompass the use of these values and attitudes in personal encounters, beyond and outside the traditional one to one counselling sessions.

Counselling Relationship

The person-centred approach, with its emphasis on an actualising or growth tendency in every living organism, is characterised by the central importance it places on the counselling relationship in order to achieve change and growth. Rogers focused on the person of the counsellor and the immediacy of the work in each session. He was anti-dogmatic and even fearful that his theories could develop into a rigid and defended set of rules, implemented by a band of clones chanting 'anything goes' and reflecting 'feeling words'! 'The person-centred approach strongly advocates openness to new insights. This can be, and frequently is, misunderstood as licence to do anything. When it is taken this way, however, the person-centred basic assumptions are likely to get lost. The demand upon the therapist to be strongly committed to the basic assumptions while simultaneously remaining anti-dogmatic can certainly be a source of confusion and dilemma'.[4]

Person-centred counselling 'is by its very nature responsive and adaptive rather than dogmatic',[5] and Rogers was always keen to deny that the counsellor possessed any mystique, or wonderful expertise, which might make her appear wise or powerful. On the contrary, he emphasised the equality and common humanity of both client and counsellor. Perhaps this book will help clients to retain their own power, their sense of self, so they can look on the work of counselling as a collaborative effort, where the person being helped can remain the 'expert' in their own lives, and yet acknowledge that they need help right now to clarify and use that expertise. 'In many ways person-centred counselling does not fit so-called Western culture ... where expertness in the pursuit of authority over others is a goal at every level of societal functioning from commerce through academia to the criminal fraternity.'[6]

Yet because the work of counselling is so intangible, so much of the moment, it is difficult for a client to stand back and remember what actually went on within a session, what was actually said, what the response was. It can be difficult to understand how something so fleeting and 'plain' can make such a profound difference to my well-being and my self-acceptance, to my sense of clarity and understanding of myself and my life.

What can at times feel like patronising comments from those working with other theories or in other disciplines (who may have a vague knowledge of core conditions and often little else) can cause person-centred counsellors to feel at times, not just misunderstood, but misrepresented. It used to be said that English was widely used internationally, in so many fields of endeavour, 'because it can so quickly be spoken so poorly. In a similar way one suspects that client-centred therapy is often taught primarily, and wrongly, because it is believed to be easy to learn.'[7] Some counsellors who would claim to be PC-oriented, state that it is good to be person-centred at the beginning of the work, but then it is important to use another theory for the 'real work'.

It is also sometimes claimed that PCA is merely a reflection of the times in which it was first outlined, but

Rogers and his theories did not burst on the world out of nowhere! He had many mentors from many disciplines, and was influenced also by Zen thinking, but his theories are firmly founded on disciplined research and practical work with clients. The accusation that this approach has not changed in the twenty years since Rogers died, nor indeed in the fifty-odd years since he first formulated his ideas is inaccurate; while the basic theory may not be fundamentally different, no amount of criticism can disguise the fact that the supporters of PCA are continually writing and debating about its concepts and that far from being out of date, or set in stone, these are being explored, expanded and explained all the time. Rogers would undoubtedly have agreed with Yalom that 'our field has a long history of remarkably able contributors who have laid deep foundations for our therapy work today.'[8] Ideas and theories come and go and revive, the words change, the references grow, but the work remains strikingly similar.

Some of these most basic ideas pop up in the most unexpected places! In Australia in the nineteenth century, a convict who had spent some considerable time tethered to a rock on a small island in Sydney Harbour, was finally sent to Norfolk Island, a convict settlement many miles off the east Australian coast. Here, under the jurisdiction of Maconochie, the controller of Norfolk Island from 1840 to 1843, he became a model prisoner. However, within a short time, the authorities 'viewing with alarm the revolutionary notions of giving prisoners a sense of worth and motivation to behave themselves'[9] replaced Maconochie, and presumably the old notions of punishment and hardship reasserted themselves. I have a suspicion that Rogers would have found much in common with Maconochie!

Criticisms

It is at times suggested that Rogers only represented white, middle-class American values, and that his theories focused on personal growth and the importance of the individual to the detriment of society at large. The suggestion here is that this focus on self is indicative of the 'me' generation, that the selfishness in us all will come to the fore, and that society will descend into chaos, with each person abandoning all rules and regulations, and merely 'doing their own thing'.

Wilkins answers these criticisms clearly and convincingly and also faces down the accusation that the person-centred approach consists only of 'tea and sympathy for the worried well' while candidly admitting that he fears that 'there is a tendency on the part of therapists to see clients as 'cured' when they think like the therapist!'[10] It is also sometimes claimed that PCA deals only with an unreal world where good will always triumph, but on the contrary 'person-centred theory does not deny the existence of evil, but explains it within its own framework'.[11] Nor was Rogers blind to the existence of evil: 'I am quite aware that out of defensiveness and inner fear individuals can and do behave in ways which are incredibly cruel, horribly destructive, immature, regressive, antisocial, hurtful.'[12] He also held firmly to the belief that the existence of evil does not preclude the possibility of change.

It is also said by some critics that person-centred counselling can foster dependency, because of the particular nature of the counselling relationship. I find this hard to accept as valid. While it is true that any form of helping can encourage some dependency for some time, and that particular clients may be more predisposed than others to becoming dependent, the nature of the relationship fostered by the person-centred counsellor is predicated on independence on the part of the client. The counsellor will not give direction or advice, but aims to focus responsibility firmly within the client. In effect the counsellor constantly reflects attitudes such as '*You* know where it hurts, *you* have the knowledge for healing, *you* can do it', thereby continually offsetting any tendency to long-term dependency on the part of the client.

Who is the counsellor?

Few people choose a career in counselling early in their working lives. Most of us come to counselling via events in our personal lives, or through allied work such as nursing or teaching. Counselling may have helped us through a crisis in the past, and we may be keen to 'give something back', recognising the value of counselling through personal experience.

My own introduction to counselling was different also. In the late nineteen forties and fifties, my husband Myles O'Farrell worked with groups of educationally deprived young men (and a very few young women), with the encouragement and support of a Jesuit priest, Fr J.P. Conran in St Francis Xavier Church in north Dublin. These young men had left school when they were twelve or thirteen and gone to work in what were, in those hungry days, valued jobs, but which were also 'dead-end'. They worked as bar-staff, hospital porters, corporation drivers, store-men; bright youngsters in jobs that required little initiative, and that for some were tedious, grinding and soul-destroying.

I came on the scene in the mid-fifties; at that time we had never heard of Carl Rogers, and counselling was not a familiar word, let alone a career. There was some marriage counselling and career guidance, but non-directive or client-centred counselling had not arrived. And yet the work Myles was doing was in essence client-centred. He believed that if a young man or woman became aware of a wish for change in his life or circumstances, the achievement of which appeared to be impossible, then with encouragement he could realise that dream, no matter how futile or unthinkable it appeared. If he had tried to describe his work, he might have said: 'if the young person can see the shimmering outline of a dream, and has the potential to fulfil it, then he can achieve it – given acceptance and encouragement within a supportive relationship'.

And it worked! The young men ranged from fourteen to twenty-five years of age, and came from a variety of backgrounds. Once they realised that someone was willing to listen to their ambitions, and believed that they could achieve them, then neither money nor opposition from home proved a deterrent. And opposition was at times quite shocking. One young medical student's books were destroyed by her parents, and efforts were made to physically prevent others from attending lectures. Irate parents accused Myles of 'leading their children astray', encouraging them to leave 'good' jobs, and there was little awareness of investing in the person's future. The small money at week's end was needed, and was more secure than any hope of riches in five years time. In the climate of unemployment and poverty and emigration of the fifties, this was a very real and understandable outlook. And yet it was difficult when potential employers offered tangible opportunities and these were turned down as 'not what his father had done' or 'aiming too high'.

The groups of twenty to thirty met weekly with Myles, and 'recruits' came by word of mouth and friends of friends. It was all voluntary and perhaps homespun, but more effective than either Myles or I could have guessed. When he died in 1975, there was a steady stream of strangers to my door to say: 'You don't know me, but your husband changed my life. I was a member of his study-group in the late forties, or fifties, and I'd like to say thank-you.' Even today I sometimes meet people who remember his particular influence.

So in 1975 it appeared to be a logical step for me to look for training in the helping field, not to try and re-create the study group, but to expand and explore for myself some of the ideas and choices about fulfilling ambitions and seeking change. There were no counselling courses on offer, so I completed a two-year post-graduate course in psychology, which incorporated a large measure of self-awareness, group work, and counselling skills. I had by now some knowledge of different counselling theories, and found client-centred counselling both the most familiar, and also conceptually the closest to the way I wished to work. From there I began in private practice, with no experience, no accreditation, because this did not then exist, and no supervision, because this concept did not exist either at the time. From today's vantage point, I both admire my temerity, and shudder at my foolhardiness!

I think what attracted me to the client-centred approach, as it was called then, rather than other theories of which I had gained some knowledge, were its basic tenets: respect for the client as an equal, acknowledgement of the worth of each person as an individual with individual differences, values, opinions, the 'non expert' role of the counsellor, and the emphasis on power being in the hands of the client. I felt it combined the universality of the actualising tendency in us all with the particularity of that potential for each individual. And this has not changed for me.

To be able now to work in a way that reflects how I try to live my own life is deeply satisfying. The future I wish for my clients is the same future I wish for myself: to be fully functioning, to make choices and accept responsibility for those choices, to reach their full potential, to be free of the burden of other people's opinions and criticisms, to live their lives with courage and with happiness.

Another Way

The path towards counselling for my colleague, Carl Berkeley, was totally different, and he relates his story in his own words:

> I first became aware of the work of Carl Rogers when I was studying psychology at Brunel University in England. I had returned to education at the grand old age of thirty-two, after a chequered life of business, both family and my own. Always feeling dissatisfied and searching for something unknown, I realised the only thing I really enjoyed was sitting having coffee and talking to people, so what better than studying the humanities ? My father had been born in Romania, and being the son of a foreigner and Jewish, and struggling with my sexual orientation, I had never felt I fitted in with either the English environment or the smaller suburban Jewish society around me.
>
> The first book by Rogers that I read was *On Becoming a Person*, and the title alone encouraged me, with its idea of the uniqueness of the individual. The basic concept of the book was acceptance of the person, of me, for who and what I was. My differences could be accepted. I then read everything available by Rogers, and in particular *The Freedom to Learn* made a deep impact. To encourage a child through his strengths, to accept him as he was without judgement and with love, was not just therapy, it was a whole way of being, and it was the way the world could

grow. In my enthusiasm I would give talks on Rogers to the rest of my class!

I felt I had to meet him, and while working in Chicago I wrote to him in California, where he lived. I am sure it was a gushing and naïve letter, but he replied to say he would meet me if and when I got there, but he hoped I wouldn't be wasting my time coming a thousand miles to see him. (I still have the letter). I expected to see a golden halo around his head (and perhaps that he would see my halo also!), but a quieter, less charismatic man you could not meet. We sat on his patio overlooking the Pacific Ocean and talked, and while it was not the meeting of great minds I had hoped for, it was encouraging and informative.

The following year I attended the Center for Studies of the Person in La Jolla, California, as my summer work placement, a seventeen-day encounter group held every year. There were 175 participants from all over the world, and we met in groups over the time allotted. There were no directions or instructions, and we spoke as the mood took us, sharing and explaining, listening, trying to understand and make space for one another. I remember telling about myself, all the toxic feelings I had stored over the years, the grief, the misery, the loneliness, the despair. I wept and sobbed and no one tried to stop me and no comment was made, but although I had showed my weak selfish self, my need for people and yet my disdain for them, nobody turned away from me. They gave me space, and still accepted me and respected me as part of the group and a worthwhile human being.

Another important lesson I learned was what it truly meant to be non-judgemental. I found myself listening to and comforting a middle-aged woman who was grieving a recent loss, and felt very close to her. Later I discovered that she was a dean in a prestigious college, and thought 'Well, she needs to sort herself out. Imagine a dean of students behaving like that'. As I heard my own critical voice, I realised how conditioned I was, expecting a successful person in authority to be less than human, and promised myself that I would in future try to accept and connect with the person, rather than with their job or their role.

At the end of the programme I remember standing on my own on a warm and clear evening, listening to the birds' evensong, and for the first time in my life not envying them their ability to fly away, to escape. Instead I was aware that they could never have the experience I was having! From then on, the core conditions of Rogers – empathy, acceptance and congruence – became for me a way of living my life, and not merely part of therapeutic practice. Obviously I did not live happily ever after, but I do believe that my life has been both easier and more contented as a result of this experience, and my way of working is bounded by these core conditions.[13]

Individual counsellors

Person-centred therapy is so personal to each counsellor, so linked to the style of the counsellor, that if each practitioner were to write a book, then they would all be very different. This would probably have been fully acceptable to Rogers, who was fearful of spawning 'disciples', who would parrot 'acceptable' responses and aim for the core conditions as if they were merely skills, thus losing entirely the main thrust of his theory, which was the requirement to be wholly and truly ourselves in the relationship. There is a vast difference between someone who has acquired communication and listening skills which reflect some of the ideas of Carl Rogers, and someone who has trained in depth in person-centred counselling. Acquiring skills and some knowledge of the core conditions can be helpful in all manner of situations and relationships, but does not equip a person to be a person-centred counsellor. This distinction seems obvious enough, but it is often not fully grasped by either counsellors or trainers, and Wilkins asks if this may be a consequence of person centred counsellors hiding our lights under bushels: 'perhaps we have preached principally to the converted'[14] by writing almost exclusively in person-centred journals. Whatever the reason, the mistaken view is often offered that person-centred counselling does not have a distinct identity, but merely provides a safe relationship within which other techniques or approaches may be used. We would do well to remember that 'person-centred counselling is extremely dangerous for practitioners who have insufficient training'[15] and I would add that it could also be extremely detrimental to the client.

There are three main aspects to Rogers' theory: his theory of personality or 'self-theory' (why we are the way we are); his theory of therapy (how we can change and help others to change); and his ideas on inter-personal relationships (how we can enhance and strengthen all our relationships). In order to be a person-centred counsellor, a working knowledge of *all three* is essential. Counsellors do not just use the first theory that comes their way, and even an over-view of different theories enables some choice to be made. We can concentrate on the theory that sits most comfortably with our values and the type of person we are, that forms a 'best-fit' with our ideas about human nature and why people behave the way they do, and how we would like to be in relation with them.

For example, I believe that many people who come for counselling operate out of a fear, perhaps unrecognised and unacknowledged, that if others could see their real selves they would shun them. Desperate for acceptance, they live a life of pretence and cover-up, portraying a self that they hope others will find acceptable. They are constantly defending themselves against discovery, and my way of working will concentrate on trying to create safety for them, so that they may begin to discard their defences in this particular relationship, acknowledge and accept their real selves, and eventually learn to live differently in the world outside the counselling room.

'By definition, people legitimately adopting the label "person-centred" have *chosen* to believe in the actualising tendency with its various implications.'[16] My reasons for choosing a particular way of working may be philosophical, psychological or religious, but at the very least they will provide me with some *raison-d'etre* for my methods. Without any such reason, I may be whistling in the dark, ready to grasp at any old method or technique, responding to my client's story and feelings as if from a void. Rogers derived his theories from observation of client-work, rather than by applying abstract theories to clients to see if they would prove accurate. For him practice took precedence over theory, without in any way minimising the importance of theory. The client's *perception* of himself and his experiences remained paramount.

> While the successful practice of person-centred therapy may depend upon the suspension of theoretical knowledge in the actual encounter, it must nevertheless be grounded in a thorough understanding of person-centred concepts... But I am quite clear that the place for theorising is during reflection, *not* in the act of relating.[17]

It is difficult to understand how some helpers, whose work it is to facilitate change, try to work without a sound theoretical background, or in a manner so eclectic that they spin like a weather-vane in their attempt to select some form of response to each client's need. It is as if they look on theory and therapy as the same thing, the 'doing' of something the same as the 'reason' for doing it. It is essential that I have some theory about human development and what causes emotional disturbance, so that I can appreciate how my clients may change. My choice of theory will inform my way of working and relating with my client, while I remain always aware that 'theorising may inform practice but it should not dictate it'.[18] *How* I work in the moment may be different with each client, but will always be within the theoretical framework of the person-centred approach.

Personal Style
Rogers himself emphasised the importance of the personal style of each counsellor, and he was emphatic that to put a counsellor into a 'methodological strait-jacket' would in no way advance the relationship between counsellor and client, and would rather hinder the exploratory work of the client. 'Thus our sharply different therapists achieve good results in quite different ways. For one, an impatient, no-nonsense, let's put-the-cards-on-the-

table approach is most effective, because in such an approach he is most openly being himself. For another it may be a much more gentle, and more obviously warm approach, because this is the way *this* therapist is.'[19] (This emphasis on the realness of the counsellor in any given moment is dealt with in the chapter on the core conditions.) However, we would do well not to take this statement as permission to merely stumble ahead with our clients, recklessly experimenting with this or that comment or response or technique, perhaps going blindly with whatever hypothesis we like at any given moment. The focus remains on the client, and on the relationship between the client and the counsellor, and how the counsellor fosters this relationship will depend on her theoretical stance. For Rogers as a teacher, imparting knowledge of theory took the form of dialogue and was never presented as doctrine or dogma. Rogers himself deplored those followers of his who not only slavishly adhered to some basic elements of his theories, but also used his ideas merely to create techniques based on automatic repetition of the client's words, and in 1961 was moved to comment: 'I have found it difficult to know, at times, whether I have been hurt more by my "friends" or my enemies.'[20]

Perhaps some at least of the need for techniques and water-tight theories stems from the insecurity and uncertainty attached to the practice of all counselling, and perhaps most of all to person-centred counselling, which relies entirely on the relationship and the person of the counsellor. Mearns titles a chapter 'What to do if you are not perfect!', which is comforting and encouraging, not just for the trainee counsellor, but for all of us who practise. He discusses the need some of us have to attain perfection, rather than to constantly strive towards it, or at least in the direction of it: 'we have emphasised that while personal development is a crucial aspect of counsellor training, ... it is perfectly possible for counsellors to forgo the attainment of perfection ... and learn the skills involved in working around areas of difficulty.'[21] There is not merely scope for combining personal development with practised counselling and listening skills, but to do so is essential if we are to become effective counsellors.

Finally, to return to the source, in 1984 Rogers gave the following definition of his theory of counselling:

> Client-centered therapy is continually developing a way of being with persons that facilitates healthy change and growth. Its central hypothesis is that persons have within themselves vast resources for self-understanding and for constructive changes in ways of being and behaving and that these resources can best be released and realised in a relationship with certain definable qualities. When therapists or other helping persons are experiencing and communicating their own realness, caring, and a deeply sensitive non-judgemental understanding, such release and change are most likely to occur. It is in moments when therapists experience empathy with their clients so deep as to become intuitive, a response by the whole organism, that major shifts occur. The quality of the relationship is central to the whole therapeutic process.[22]

Notes

1. Carl Rogers quoted in *The Carl Rogers Reader*, eds Howard Kirschenbaum and Valerie Land Henderson.
2. Brian Thorne *Carl Rogers* (Sage, 1992) vii.
3. Dave Mearns and Brian Thorne *Person-Centred Counselling in Action* (Sage, 1999).

4. David Brazier, ed. *Beyond Carl Rogers* (Constable, 1993) 275.
5. Paul Wilkins *Person-Centred Therapy in Focus* (Sage, 2003) 28.
6. Dave Mearns *Developing Person-Centred Counselling* (Sage, 1994) ix
7. David Brazier, ed. *Beyond Carl Rogers* (Constable, 1993) 279.
8. Irvin D. Yalom *The Gift of Therapy* (Piatkus, 2001) 2.
9. Angela Long, review in the *Irish Times* (28 July 2001) of *Maconchie's Experiment* by John Clay, published by John Murray, 2001.
10. Paul Wilkins *Person-Centred Therapy in Focus* (Sage, 2003) 24.
11. Martin Van Kalmthout 'Personality Change and the Concept of the Self' in *Person Centred Therapy; a European perspective* (Sage, 1998) 56.
12. Carl Rogers *On Becoming A Person* (Houghton Mifflin, 1961) 27.
13. Personal statement to author.
14. Paul Wilkins *Person-Centred Therapy in Focus* (Sage, 2003) 2.
15. Dave Mearns *Developing Person-Centred Counselling Training* (Sage, 1997) x.
16. Paul Wilkins *Person-Centred Therapy in Focus* (Sage, 2003) 14.
17. Ibid., 46.
18. Ibid., 40.
19. Carl Rogers quoted in *Beyond Carl Rogers* ed. David Brazier (Constable) 22.
20. Carl Rogers *On Becoming A Person* (Houghton Mifflin, 1961) 15.
21. Dave Mearns Developing *Person-Centred Counselling* (Sage, 1994) 37-9.
22. C.R. Rogers & Ruth Sanford 'Client Centred-Psychotherapy' in *Comprehensive Textbook of Psychiatry IV*, eds H.I. Kaplan and B. J. Sadcock (Williams and Wilkins Company, 1984) 1374.

2

Self-Actualisation

'There is an Indian proverb or axiom that says that everyone is a house with four rooms, a physical, a mental, an emotional and a spiritual. Most of us tend to live in one room most of the time but, unless we go into every room every day, even if only to keep it aired, we are not a complete person.'[1]

Actualising tendency

One of the main tenets of the person-centred approach is the belief in the actualising tendency, which is the basic, natural tendency in all organisms to fulfil their potential. In an ideal world, without obstacles or disasters, the organism would proceed towards becoming all that is in-built in its structure. It would fulfil its potential. This potential is the person's personal blueprint, encompassing their hereditary traits, genetic markers, their inherent potentialities and capabilities. From his work with clients, Rogers perceived within the human person a fundamental drive, 'an underlying flow of movement toward constructive fulfilment of its inherent possibilities. The behaviours of an organism can be counted on to be in the direction of maintaining, enhancing, and reproducing itself.'[2]

However, obstacles to complete fulfilment being inevitable, the organism has to struggle to achieve this growth, yet, although thwarted and almost buried, the spark of this impulse remains alive. Rogers believed that only the death or destruction of the organism could fully extinguish this actualising tendency.

Selective and directional, this is a basic biological concept, neither 'good' nor 'bad', which impels the individual towards self-authority, self-determination and growth. The underlying premise is that the human person is essentially constructive rather than destructive. The theory does not state that human nature is all sweetness and light, incapable of aggressive behaviour, as is sometimes claimed by critics of PCA. It rather 'sees destructive behaviour and feelings simply as manifestations of the person ... functioning *under unfavourable conditions*.'[3] In other words, the essentially constructive person reacts aggressively and destructively when the impulse to grow and develop is threatened.

The Self and the self-image

The definition of 'Self' forms the basis for much on-going discussion within the person-centred tradition. The self is not fixed or immutable, yet 'at any given moment it is a specific entity',[4] 'self is that which endures through the flux of life... associated with traditional ideas of immortal soul'.[5] It is not an isolated entity, but one which is fluid and flexible, intertwined with other people and subject to both the actualising tendency and the restraints of social interaction. Zohar writes: 'we see the self as a fluctuating and fuzzy thing whose boundaries, both internal and external, are always shifting and changing.'[6]

My 'Self' then is my real 'ME', my organismic fundamental being.

My 'self-concept' is the knowledge, idea or picture I have of my self.

My 'self-image' is the picture (often false) which I present to others in order to win their approval. It can be so powerful that I may forget that it is a false image, consisting of masks and pretences, and I may come to believe that it is my true self.

When a baby is born, her organismic self is her basic core self, her identity as a unique person in her own right. To begin with, the child knows clearly what she likes and dislikes. Her source of evaluation is clearly within herself, and she reacts to evidence supplied by her senses. She is hungry and she cries; she is cuddled and she smiles.

She develops an awareness of her own self as separate from others, and begins to differentiate some of her experiences, she interacts with her environment and significant others. However, as awareness of self emerges, and while her self-concept is being formed, a potent need becomes apparent in the infant, a need for positive regard from others. 'This need is universal in human beings, and in the individual is pervasive and persistent',[7] and so powerful that it can over-ride the full expression of the actualising tendency and the person's valuing process.

This self-concept can match fairly well with the organismic real self, and if others accept and love the baby, this match can remain close. The positive reactions from others give the child a positive picture of herself, a positive self-concept, and she will grow up feeling that she is loveable and acceptable – to others at first, and by degrees to herself. Her self-image which she portrays to others, corresponds fairly well with the way she sees herself, with her self-concept. Believing she is loved and accepted, she can love and accept herself. A student once described herself as having been brought up hearing constantly that she was 'a golden girl', and she still believed this, and felt she was a special and loveable person. Both her self-concept and her self-image were very positive, and similar. She was able to deal with her world as a confident and self-aware person.

This self-concept fluctuates, positive today, negative tomorrow, but through all these changes and shifts, it can be defined at any given moment. It includes my perception of my own characteristics, my relationships with other people and other aspects of living, and the values attached to these. 'Self-concept is the person's conceptual construction of himself (however poorly expressed).'[8]

This is one end of the continuum and there are obviously many degrees and variations of acceptance by others. To begin with the child trusts and acts out of her own experience, but in time learns that such 'true' response does not always have the desired effect of winning positive regard. As this need for positive regard from others becomes paramount, it meets with negativity as well as with positive reactions, and can also be selective or inconsistent, creating confusion around the self-concept. If others criticise, disapprove, neglect, then this negativity causes anxiety and distress, and a negative self-concept is formed, modelled on the perceived attitudes of others, rather than on a reflection of her own experiences. She begins to believe that she is unloveable, unacceptable, worthless, bcause she perceives others as not loving or accepting her real self. She begins to behave 'as she *should* rather than as she actually does feel and would like to behave.'[9] The child tries to foster those behaviours in herself which she sees as winning love from those who are important to her, perhaps by being quiet, well-behaved, not crying, and so on.

As the child tries to project an image of a self that will be loved and accepted, her self-concept too may alter as she strives to persuade herself that she really *is* the person she is trying to be, and the gap between the real self and the false self-concept/image widens to a point where they are often in conflict. As the need for protection from negativity increases, the voice of the real self becomes fainter. It may eventually fall silent and the negative 'people-pleasing' self-concept/image becomes dominant. Man 'deserts his own experiencing to take on the way of being that will bring love.'[10] It is very often such a negative self-concept/image which brings people into counselling for a kind of therapeutic re-education.

Our real, basic self therefore can be over-laid with a concept of self, constructed to deny our real selves. We believe that the love of others is conditional on 'acceptable' behaviour, that important others will love us 'only' if we behave as they would wish, and then we strive to become that other loveable self. We hide away and conceal the real self which we believe will not find acceptance. We construct a false self-concept and we show the world a false image of ourselves.

Conditions of worth
Individuals, therefore, can be thwarted in their self-actualisation by their interactions with significant others in their lives, and will not only strive to manifest those qualities they perceive as more 'acceptable' to others, but will at the same time try to suppress the person they are who is at times bold, loud, bad-mannered. The child perceives others as having laid down 'conditions' required for her to be a person of some worth, and models her self-concept on what she believes others would like her to be, since their approval and love is all-important. She comes to believe that she is only

loveable and worthwhile if she is manifesting the accepted behaviour. She values herself only in so far as she is the model of what is required, or what she sees as required by others. From this pervasive need for positive regard from others evolves the need for self-regard, which becomes similarly selective. To learn to regard ourselves positively is understandably difficult if those around us are critical or disapproving.

The child adopts those attitudes of others, which were seen as either positive or negative, to a valuing system which leads to positive or negative *self*-regard. These conditions of worth have been expanded from being a measure of how others regarded her to encompass how she values herself. Using the same criteria for worthiness, loveableness, as she perceived others to apply, she regards herself as worth-while, or not.

The individual then has created for herself a negative self-concept, which constantly demands that she present herself to the world as something other than her 'real' self, a false self-image which is constantly reinforced by an inner critical voice, measuring, chiding, undermining. She has low self-esteem. She will have little or no belief in her own judgement, and her 'locus (or place) of evaluation', the measure of her value as a human being, will have become based in others rather than within herself. This locus of evaluation is the decider of what is right or wrong, what might be wise to do or not do, and her behaviour is governed by the opinion of others. So powerful and so potent is this need to conform to what is perceived to be expected, that it can be stronger even than the actualising tendency. The person's valuing system for all her daily living, and the decisions she makes, have been firmly placed in the keeping of others. The 'Joneses' are the deciders, and her life is not free.

One of the effects of this is that her perception of experiences becomes distorted, with those experiences which match her conditions of worth being reflected in her awareness, but those which are contrary being denied to her awareness or altered. She does not include these in her self-picture, which is based on information from outside herself and valued according to an external locus of evaluation. Her self-concept needs constant protection from the threat of her real self, which would be unacceptable to others. New experiences are dangerous and change is always negatively perceived. She is defending her self-concept from change. A threatening experience, a memory-trace from the past, an impulse of rage towards a person in authority, may be blocked from entering her awareness, although the incongruence thus experienced, and perhaps only dimly perceived, generates anxiety and some awareness of danger may leak in.

We can have real difficulty in communicating between 'both aspects of our divided self – our conscious façade and our deeper level of understanding.'[11] Holding the balance can be costly and difficult, and conflict and tension between the two create dissonance and disturbance in the psyche, which can even break down at times of stress, such as death or loss. While my defences can protect my acceptable self-concept during my day-to-day living, experiences which highlight the hidden contradictions can undermine and even shatter the carefully maintained border between my self-picture and my actual experience, my real self.

Rogers wrote of this 'fundamental rift' between our real selves and our image of ourselves. We sense 'one meaning in experience, but the conscious self clings rigidly to another, since that is the way it has found love and acceptance from others.'[12] If the person could be fully open to the experience, it would be available to awareness, in the immediate lived-in moment, and could be dealt with there and then. A point may be reached where maintaining the mask of the false self is demanding too much effort and energy. Perhaps the individual is racked by depression or panic attacks. If my defences crumble, then inner tensions and anxiety result, which can be experienced as 'threatening to the self without any awareness of the content of that threat. Such anxiety is often seen in therapy as the individual approaches awareness of some element of his experience which is in sharp contradiction to his self-concept.'[13] What is needed is a kind of 'deconstruction of old constructions.'[14]

Role of the counsellor

The false picture, therefore, can become a form of control, by outside forces, over the wants and desires and needs of the person, and the counsellor aims to help the client to unravel 'the "personal theory" he has constructed around his own experiencing.'[15] A client geared from childhood to fulfil and satisfy a parent's wishes, can be governed by a concept of herself as having one purpose in life, and one only, that of serving her mother's or her father's needs. Her own wishes and emotions are always so secondary that they merit hardly a second thought. Indeed, they can become almost unknown to the person who, then or later in life, if asked 'What would you like to do? Which would you choose?' falls into a state of confusion and indecision. Her knowledge, or her awareness of her real organismic self has been so overlaid by the need to fulfil other people's demands that she has practically lost all sight of what it is she *would* like to do. Hence she has no habit or history of weighing the merits or demerits of a course of action, of making an informed choice. There appears to be no choice available for her, no freedom of decision, merely the pleasing of, or agreeing with the other. Making one's own decisions can be quite fearful to contemplate, not only because it is unaccustomed, but also because it brings with it the responsibility for these decisions, and for the mistakes which may follow. 'Freedom is ... permeated with anxiety'[16] because in order to achieve real and lasting change, it is essential that individuals recognise that they have had a role in creating their difficulties. Having come to this realisation it is almost a logical step towards becoming aware that they also have the power to change their situation.

The nature of the work within person-centred counselling depends to a great extent on the client's locus of evaluation. Where it is firmly placed within myself, then I can feel more free to explore and to challenge. With a client whose valuing system is clearly based in other people, it would be wise to remain constantly aware of this client's vulnerability to even a hint or suggestion of direction towards decision or action. It would be all too easy for me to become yet another person that my client had to cajole or please.

In order to facilitate this re-drafting of a client's self-knowledge and self-direction, the counsellor herself needs to be integrated and self-aware. The impact of clients can be very strong, and is imperative that she have a strong resilient self-image and a positive self-awareness, partly to model openness in relationships, but also to remain her own true self in the complex and shifting nuances of this counselling relationship. A client's turmoil can threaten to engulf us as counsellors, so we need to be able to enter the client's world while remaining intact, not defensive and not en-shelled, but open and willing to share of ourselves without losing our integrity as our own self. For example, I find one of the most difficult emotions to stay with is my client's loneliness. The impulse to offer something more than counselling can be very strong. Rogers identifies two elements in the loneliness so often seen in our clients. 'The first is the estrangement of man from himself', between the real self and the false self created to please others, and the second is our inability 'to communicate both aspects of our divided self' to another in a relationship. We are not able to 'communicate our real experiencing – and hence our real self – to another.'[17] Obviously a lack of awareness of our feelings and the consequent inability to express our feelings are detrimental to all relationships. The hoped-for outcome of counselling is that, in laying aside the masks and defences, and becoming more of her real self, my client will be able to share herself more fully and more honestly in her dealings with others. This could not be readily achieved if my pain and concern for this lonely person were to leak into our relationship, within which the client will find her own solutions.

It is important also to remember that our image of ourself is not consistent, nor is it singular, and that the material presented by the client, and her attitude towards the counsellor, can vary from day to day. The possibility of altering her self-concept, her false self, of bringing it closer to her real self, can be achieved through a greater understanding of this self-concept, because this knowledge can be utilised to alter her attitudes and self-directed behaviour, resulting in the awareness of the person she really is.

'The therapist is offering a unique opportunity – a person who is willing and able to relate at depth with *all* the parts of the client.'[18] People often speak of their 'selves' as almost distinct from the 'self' they show to the world. 'If people saw my real self, they wouldn't like me', 'I was beside myself with rage', 'There is a part of me that is very sad, but I just cannot go there', 'It's as if there's this needy little boy inside who comes out to look for attention.' These different and inconsistent parts of ourselves are named 'configurations' by Mearns and Thorne[19] and they speak of a 'whole constellation of configurations'. (Terms with somewhat similar meanings in other forms of therapy include ego states, subpersonalities, voices within, sub-selves.) These configurations are accessible to the client's conscious process, and their importance lies not merely in their particularity, but also in the interactions between the different 'characters' in my inner theatre. These differing 'selves' may be merely labels for the conflict within the client's personality and 'the person-centred counsellor's task is to manifest the therapeutic conditions in relation to *all* the aspects of the personality',[20] both growthful and not-for-growth configurations. It is essential that counsellors accept equally both the client who appears to be firmly 'stuck' in an unmoving and repetitive place, and the client who appears to be forging ahead with life changes. This can be particularly difficult for counsellors at the beginning of their career, who seek reassurance from their ability to 'move the client along' and thus measure 'progress'.

Authority of the client

Mearns and Thorne refer to two models within educational policy, a deficiency model and a potentiality model. The deficiency model suggests that the learner is 'deficient' and must be rendered more efficient by the input of knowledge or skills, while the potentiality model suggests that 'the learner has a huge array of potentialities manifested in embryonic skills and talents.'[21] These can be highlighted and encouraged, and PCA shares with most other forms of therapy both the practice and the language of the potentiality model. To try and uncover the buried real self becomes the shared task of client and counsellor.

The drive towards fulfilling our potential, therefore, can be thwarted or impeded by obstacles such as conflict, stress, illness, and so on, and my task as person-centred counsellor is to help the client to re-instate this drive. Belief in this actualising tendency enables me to trust each client to find his own way and make his own decisions; this trust is fundamental to the person-centred approach. The authority for the person is centred within the client herself, and not within the counsellor. My client is responsible for her own feelings, behaviours, thoughts, and my responsibility is to be as good a counsellor as I can, while allowing clients to go in their own direction and at their own pace. I do not accept the idea of an outside 'expert', although I have expertise in the general field of counselling. My basic assumption is that the client, and only the client, is the authority on the world of the client. The client's perception of herself, rather than my perception of her, is where the emphasis lies, since I see my main function as enabling or facilitating the actualising process of my client.

As we saw earlier, this actualising process moves in the direction of growth and fulfilment of the inherent potentiality of the person. Clients can invest their counsellor with 'expertise', but I do not have to accept this. My message should be one of equality and respect for the person, and I will constantly hand back the proffered power and authority.

'An important and distinguishing feature of person-centred therapy is that it does not drift into the unconscious but works within the awareness and, we are suggesting, the *emerging* awareness of the client.'[22] Obviously this is not to deny the existence of the unconscious (that would be foolish indeed), but the focus is on material which is known to the client, and where he may be 'expert'.

They go further: 'The unconscious world of the client as it is "explored" in therapy is, in fact, a combination of the *therapist's* theoretical constructions and the *therapist's* imagination.'[23]

If it is accepted that the 'client knows where it hurts' and if this is what I work with, then material present in the unconscious is not available to the person and will not be included in their current knowledge of their self. This edge-of-awareness, 'subceived' material can influence behaviour, as well as cause anxiety. Some memory just below awareness for this client may be nudging into consciousness in response perhaps to a word or a thought. It is at times plainly visible, for example where the client unwittingly uses a word or phrase which sounds to the counsellor like a step beyond what has been mentioned up to now. When highlighted or repeated by the counsellor, the client may express surprise as to 'where that came from', but it is the client who explains or expands or interprets, not the counsellor. A client of mine, having mentioned a particular song, said: 'I hate it. I don't know why but it always tears me up inside.' Exploration of the sadness associated with the music revealed a hitherto blocked-out memory which changed her perception of a previous and important event in her life.

Human beings have a great and unique potential for learning about their own nature and for moving in the direction of positive self-realisation. The person-centred counsellor believes that people will go in their own directions, choose their own ways and make their own decisions, no matter what advice or solutions might be suggested. The counsellor who begins to believe that she knows better than this 'poor client' concerning what is 'good' for him, and in what direction he needs to go, is not only dealing poorly with that client, but is also herself in trouble. The role of all-knowing and all-wise counselling guru is sadly ineffective.

And while it sounds straightforward, it is all too easy to become focused on our own vision of what is good for this client, on our solution to their unhappiness. Based on a cursory knowledge of the difficulties involved, we can lose sight of the self-determination of our clients, and become fixers or solvers. The challenge for the counsellor is whether I can 'allow' or tolerate this locus of control to remain with the client, and to permit this client to be sad, or angry, or stuck, without feeling impelled to intrude with my own solutions or interpretations. Perhaps I cannot tolerate the level of sadness any longer, and feel impelled to interpret or 'fix' the problem. Perhaps I am impatient and tired of hearing the same story over and over. I want 'to move the client along'. This can create a situation where 'the self-authority and the self-determination of the client is undermined by the seeping authority of the therapist.'[24]

Working thus within the parameters of the client's actualising tendency enlists the client on her own behalf. The client works within his own perception of his self and his world, rather than trying to fit himself into someone else's picture, or trying to please the counsellor by being a 'good' client. This enables the client to retrieve a true picture of his self, and to begin to eschew the false 'people pleasing' self-images on which he has been relying up to now. This can be a very frightening endeavour. It is no longer the emperor who has no clothes, but me, myself, being revealed without trappings or disguises. 'The greater the extent that therapists honor the authority of clients as the authority of their own lives then the greater the probability of constructive personality change and problem resolution'.[25]

Basically then it is required of the person-centred counsellor that she trust in the person, the client, to know 'where it hurts', and to know further what is required to change and to heal. 'I have not found counselling or therapy effective when I have tried to create in another individual something that is not already there'.[26] The counsellor needs to believe that people can change – if they want to, and that self-actualisation is the motive for change. The basic fundamental qualities of the human person are growth, process and change. 'To be that self one truly is means a self which is flexible, not fixed'.[27]

Self-acceptance

If I manage to convey my continued acceptance of my client, then he will begin to see the possibility of accepting himself, as a person valued by the counsellor, and therefore as a person of at least *some* value. He no longer sees himself as worthless and to be despised, but as a person who has both strengths and weaknesses, who is also a person of some worth. My acceptance of my client as a valuable and unique person in his own right is played in counter-point to the older message of 'I will only love and accept you if you meet my conditions of worth.' The possibility of altering the false self, of bringing it closer to the real self, can be achieved through understanding the self-concept, because this knowledge can be utilised to alter attitudes and self-directed behaviour, resulting in the awareness of the person we really are.

Through this acceptance and through 'the releasing of emotional blocks which have locked the client, perhaps for years, in a negative view of herself'[28], the client is increasingly able to contact and express his feelings and wishes, and reference them to himself, rather than to his non-self. The actor Billy Connolly's mock-serious comment: 'One loves one' illustrates how feelings are often expressed at a safe remove from the speakers real self, and here the distancing from reality is further exaggerated as the feeling is addressed to the non-self of the loved one! By identifying and re-experiencing his deeply hidden emotional world, the client is able to own and express his feelings, thereby defusing their power to threaten him. And since it is a fundamental tenet of the PCA that 'our behaviour is to a large extent an acting-out of the way we actually feel about ourselves and the world we inhabit';[29] acknowledging and owning our feelings enables us to change our behaviour if we wish.

A gap can also open up between our inherent separateness and our need for connection with others. Clients with powerful conditions of worth are often sacrificing actualisation to the social demands and structures of their lives. 'It is a fundamental drive within us to make the most we can of our living process and much of that living process is social in nature.'[30] The social imperative, the need to be a member of our 'social life space' may be contrary to actions which our self-actualisation would prompt. Our potential growth may be in direct opposition to our relationship needs. As a client once explained to me: 'I'd really like to stop drinking and do something different from going to the pub, but I'm afraid of losing all my friends.' It is important to 'recognise both our need for autonomy and our need for belongingness.'[31] This can be clearly seen when, for example, a client stays in an abusive relationship despite being aware of how damaging it is. The actualising tendency would suggest that she leave the situation and become free to be her own self, but the social ingredient may hold messages which suggest that being alone would be worse: I couldn't survive on my own, to be married means status, and so on.

The actualising tendency within each of us, seeking our development and growth, is therefore in dialogue with the social restraints and rules for social living, and we seek to strike a balance between these two. Too often this dialogue falters, and either the actualising tendency or the social demands predominate to the detriment of the other. For example, a client may wish to become a more real and genuine person, but the imperative of her place within a critical and competitive family may render such a choice very threatening. She may decide to remain the sister/daughter 'who can always be relied on', and have little life of her own. Where a balance cannot be re-struck to meet changing circumstances, then the result may be one of 'dis-order' and the organism struggles to find a new accommodation between its own actualising needs and the rules and demands of social living (This idea of balance needs also to be kept in mind for clients who flourish in counselling, and eventually swing wildly and totally towards self-actualisation! They may lose awareness of other people's rights and needs, and focus entirely on their 'new' selves. They are ignoring the demands of their *social* selves and are not even aware of the need to accommodate both self-actualisation and social demands.)

Acceptance of self can liberate the client from the urgent need to be what others might wish, and permits him to relate to others in a more balanced way, and to no longer fear being controlled or hurt by them. Our real self is in process: *'Life, at its best, is a flowing, changing process in which nothing is fixed.'*[32] And while this flexibility frees the client from the constraints of pleasing others, it can also be very frightening for a person emerging from a lifetime of rules and fixed structures. The old ways of surveying and interacting with our world served deeply-rooted emotional needs, and affected our feelings, thoughts and behaviours. It requires patience on the part of the counsellor, and courage on the part of the client, to explore and discuss change, never mind the actual changing. Small wonder that some clients look at the possibility of changing and then 'snatch defeat from the jaws of victory'![33]

Outcome of counselling

The hoped-for outcome of counselling is that the client will become what Rogers described as 'the fully-functioning person', or perhaps more accurately a person who functions more fully than before. There is no 'happy-ever-after' outcome available, but the person will be changed as a result. (Similarily the counsellor will be changed to some degree. It is not possible to be in relationship with another person without some impact.) The client may not be 'actualised', but they are in the process of actualising. The change is a process rather than an arrival, 'a direction, not a destination.'[34] The 'fully functioning' person will be increasingly open to, and adaptable to, her feelings and reactions in the present, and she will be less fearful and therefore less defensive. She will be more capable of trusting her own inner reactions and being her own locus of evaluation. Instead of being pulled by the expectations and demands of others, she will have fewer conditions of worth and will experience unconditional self-regard. She will embrace new situations creatively, and be free to make her own choices. Obviously this is what counselling is *aiming* to achieve, at least to some degree.

Yvonne Smith described her growth thus: 'I have learned this year to stop fighting. To stop fighting my fear, my grief and my past. It has been a difficult thing to do and was a case of learning. I survived by fighting and I felt the risk was huge to try it any other way but by reminding myself I have moved from surviving my past to living with it, which enables me to be different in the world. Embracing instead of fighting both the emotional and physical pain has made a huge difference and has greatly enhanced my life'.[35]

Instead of using adjectives such as happy or contented, Rogers felt that words like exciting, challenging, rewarding were more fitting to describe this fully functioning person, living his life as he would choose.[36] Being fully-functioning is not an ideal state to be arrived at: it is '...a directional development, not a state of being'.[37] We are, all of us, in the process of becoming, tending towards actualisation.

Notes

1. Rumer Godden *A House with Four Rooms* (Macmillan, 1989) 13.
2. Carl Rogers *A Way of Being* (Houghton Mifflin, 1980) 117-8.
3. Brian Thorne *Person-Centred Counselling* (Whurr Publications, 1991) 171.
4. Dave Mearns and Brian Thorne *Person-Centred Therapy Today* (Sage, 2000) 174.
5. David Brazier, ed., *Beyond Carl Rogers* (Constable, 1993) 83.
6. D. Zohar quoted in *Person-Centred Therapy in Focus* by Paul Wilkins (Sage, 2003) 31.
7. Howard Kirschenbaum and Valerie Land Henderson, eds., *The Carl Rogers Reader* (Constable, 1990) 245.
8. Dave Mearns and Brian Thorne *Person-Centred Counselling in Action* (Sage, 1995) 7.
9. Ursula O'Farrell *Courage to Change* (Veritas, 1999) 18.
10. Kirschenbaum and Land Henderson *The Carl Rogers Reader* 158.
11. Ibid., 157.
12. Ibid., 157.
13. Ibid., 223.
14. Adam Phillips *Promises, Promises* (Faber and Faber, 2000) 205.
15. Mearns and Thorne *Person-Centred Counselling in Action* 5.
16. Irvin D. Yalom *The Gift of Therapy* (Piatkus, 2002) 137.

17. Kirschenbaum and Land Henderson *The Carl Rogers Reader* 157.
18. Mearns and Thorne *Person-Centred Therapy Today* 103.
19. Ibid., 115.
20. Dave Mearns *Developing Person-Centred Counselling* (Sage, 1994) 15.
21. Mearns and Thorne *Person-Centred Therapy Today* 33.
22. Ibid., 176
23. Ibid., 176.
24. Jerold D. Bozarth *Person-Centered Therapy: A Revolutionary Paradigm* (PCCS Books, 1998) 87.
25. Ibid., 117.
26. Rogers *A Way of Being* 120.
27. Brian Thorne and Elke Lambers, eds., *Person-Centred Therapy – A European Perspective* (Sage, 1998) 61.
28. Mearns and Thorne *Person-Centred Counselling in Action* 149.
29. Ibid., 7.
30. Thorne and Lambers, eds., *Person-Centred Therapy – A European Perspective* 53.
31. Ibid., 53.
32. Carl Rogers *On Becoming a Person* (Constable, 1961) 27.
33. Mearns and Thorne *Person-Centred Therapy Today* 111.
34. Kirschenbaum and Land Henderson *The Carl Rogers Reader* 411.
35. Yvonne Smith – personal statement to author.
36. Kirschenbaum and Land Henderson *The Carl Rogers Reader* 142.
37. Wilkins *Person-Centred Therapy in Focus* 52.

3

Liam

'Clients, after all, have the right to remain at the level of functioning they choose without being coerced by counsellors who are bent on producing fully-functioning persons and nothing less.'[1]

Liam

When he came to counselling Liam was thirty-six years old and had been married to Jean for eight years. They have three children, Aengus, April and Anthony, at the time aged five years, three years, and eight months respectively. He had a job as a manager in a city centre store. When making his appointment, Liam said that he wanted to be better able to manage his money. He just could not pay his bills and was constantly in a state of financial chaos. As a result his marriage was suffering. In fact, his wife said that if he did not go for counselling she would leave him, taking the children.

Session 1

Liam came in, looking uneasy and shamefaced. I introduced myself, shook hands and asked him to sit down. I said we had an hour together, that whatever we discussed would be confidential (unless the safety of a third party was concerned) and invited him to tell me why he had come.

Liam: A friend of mine came to you for a few sessions last year, and he said he'd got great help, so I just thought…

I waited, because to rush in at this stage might suggest that if he couldn't speak up and speak out, I would become impatient. I wanted to let him know that he could tell his story in his own time and in his own way.

Liam: I really don't know why I've come, it's so stupid. I've got to do it myself. No-one can help.

Liam looked at the floor, at the furniture, anywhere but at me. He shifted in his chair, cleared his throat, shuffled his keys.

Me: I know it's not easy.

Liam: No. No it's not. I don't know where to begin. I feel stupid. I suppose it's about money. Not that I don't have any. Don't worry, you'll get paid! I just don't seem to be able to handle my money. Bills come in at all times of the year, and I panic when I see them, so I pick them up off the mat and just put them in a drawer in the hall. That's what I've always done. Jean, my wife, used to find them and sort them out and get me to write a cheque, but lately she's too busy, so she just throws them at me and expects me to sort them out. And then when I don't, there's a row and I'm getting really fed up with the rows. I suppose you'll tell me I should go to a 'money manager', or an accountant, or get lessons in home economics. It's just not that simple.

There was quite a lot of hostility in Liam. The assurance that I'd get my money came with the suggestion in his voice that perhaps that was all I was interested in, and the presumption that I'd suggest it was a simple matter of learning a few bookkeeping skills was not based on anything I had said. I was finding it difficult to warm to this abrasive man.

Me: Tell me more about your difficulty with bills.

Liam: Well, I know I'd pay them eventually, but I can't stand the way they keep on and on sending reminders, leaning on me, even the postman must know I owe money! Let them wait a bit longer if they're going to hassle me.

Despite the resentment, I was aware that it wasn't directed against me, but against the world, which was 'hassling' him. Feeling hard done by, and at this moment in the vulnerable position of having to look for help, I felt Liam was striking out at all and sundry. If I could accept that he was angry, and stay with him in the anger without responding in annoyance myself, then hopefully he would reach beyond it to the fear or worry or whatever was fuelling his anger. Only when he did this would he be aware of his true concerns and come to be able to do something about them.

Liam continued for the remainder of the session railing against the world and those who sought to do him down. His words appeared in part to be aimed at holding me at bay, lest anything I might say would accuse him, or distract him, or cause him to look below the surface of what he was saying. It was much too early for him to even begin to trust me.

Me: Our time is up for today, and hopefully you now have some idea of how we can work. If we could agree to meet for six sessions, and then look at how we are getting on?

Liam: (Startled) I hadn't realised it was that time. Yeah, sure. Six sessions sounds fine. Are you going to give me homework, or something to do?

The mention of homework suggested that Liam saw me as a kind of teacher, perhaps criticising or instructing, setting tasks and measuring the results.

Me: No. No homework. (I smiled as I said this, and his relief was comical, but there was also something of disappointment. Perhaps homework appeared to be something concrete, something measureable which if fulfilled, would magically improve matters.) I look forward to seeing you next week, at the same time.

I like to contract at the beginning for six sessions, as I feel that is sufficient time for us both to know if we can, or are willing, to work together. Lack of such a commitment could lead a client to decide not to come again, or change his mind about the whole enterprise. Of course he may decide to end at any time, but after only a session or two he would be deciding on a very slight experience of the process or the relationship. Six sessions forms a good 'taster' on which to make a decision to end or to continue. However, sometimes clients hear only the words 'six sessions', and assume that this is all you are pepared to allow them. They may then try to tailor their work, and their trust, to this short period. I now find myself, either in the third or fourth session, repeating my willingness to work further if *my client* wishes.

Liam presented himself as 'unlikeable' and hostile, and this is not unusual. Coming for counselling, admitting that you need help, having to disclose information about yourself, is never easy. If I can retain a sense of the basic, organismic person within, hurt, fearful, ashamed, then usually this focus persists as the outer disagreeable behaviour dissipates.

Session 5
In the previous four sessions, Liam has told me how he ignores bills, and just puts them in a drawer. He has a good salary, as he is six years in his job, but he listed endless expenses, and how the bank manager was leaning on them. He hasn't really touched on his relationship with Jean other than 'there was a fierce row', or 'she goes on and on.'

Liam: I got talking to the accountant at work today – I know him quite well. I mentioned something about how hard it is to keep track of money, and about how there's always someone ready to fleece you. Anyway he offered to give me a hand with organising what he called 'money in, money out', and it sounded great. I'm not sure if I'll go along with it, perhaps it would be mixing home and work too much, but it was good to hear him offer. Perhaps the world is full of people like me who can't manage!

Me: It sounds as if it was good to share with him, and that he was really willing to help.

Liam appeared to have shifted somewhat on the money front, which, while difficult, was safely outside of himself, 'other' than himself. Discussing his difficulties with me, even for so short a time, appeared to have given Liam the courage to mention it to his colleague. A story once told is less difficult to repeat. I hoped he was not going to decide that he had found a solution to money problems, and that therefore everything else in his life was fine and needed no more examination or change. From the little information he had given me about his relationship with Jean, I sensed there was a lot more to his difficulties and unhappiness than merely trouble with bills. Their rows were increasing, and Jean appeared to be extravagant and not a very good manager of money either. He feels she spends a lot on the house and they do not go on holidays. She goes with the children to her parents. He feels that she puts him down, in public as well as in front of the children. However, it would be his choice whether to go or to stay.

Liam: But Jean thinks I should be able to do it myself. And she's always short, and clothes and so on for the kids cost so much. Other people manage. Her nieces and nephews are always well turned out and they go on expensive holidays. And she says we need a second car, and not just another old banger. That's not fair. It's only six years old.

Me: It sounds as if it's really hard to manage.

I tried hard not to allow any sympathy with Jean and the children to intrude, because they were not here and I could not know how they might feel about the situation. Liam was my client and my focus.

Liam: We never get a night out and the people we know go to such expensive places. Everyone seems to have more money and they all look down on us.

Me: You feel other people look down on you.

Liam: Yeah! They're better managers or something, and they seem to be able to organise everything. I really feel I'm not worth much.

It is not often that clients state so clearly their lack of self-worth, and Liam seemed to arrive at this point by talking of 'money worth'.

Me: You really don't feel worth much – you feel that everyone else is worth more?

Liam: Jean says it a lot – 'you're hopeless, you're worthless.' Last night we had a huge row. I got out of the house and went down to the harbour. She's right, I can't manage. I don't know why I keep on trying. I can't satisfy anyone.

This was a difficult session to end. I had been allowing him to continue to tell his story, and merely responded to show I was hearing him. It felt too early to question his misery, and certainly useless to offer any solutions. It was difficult not to reassure Liam that it would get better, that he was a 'worthwhile' person. He sounded so despondent and hopeless, and his self-image was very negative.

Sessions 6-10 were filled with examples of how everyone else was 'better', and what they were all doing to Liam. His depressed anger was focused almost entirely on the targets of his anger, rather than on the source of that anger – himself. I had done little beyond listening closely, seeking clarification and responding where necessary. There was something about the more confident, settled way Liam came in for session 11 which suggested that he was ready to change direction or focus.

Session 11

Liam: I really want to talk about a holiday. Jean said she wanted to go and visit her parents in the country. It's her mother's sixtieth birthday in three weeks, and we've been asked. I haven't visited for ages, I don't really like them, and they sure as hell don't like me. But I'm not so sure. Birthdays are very important. I remember one year when I was eight, my dad was to bring home a cake and when he came in late, he'd been drinking, and he just said he forgot. I was gutted. Cried for a week. So I said I'd think about it and see if I could get time off work. And Jean lit up, delighted, and then of course I felt obligated and trapped, and I wonder if I should make up an excuse and say I'll be too busy after all. What do you think?

It is very tempting to give ready answers when appealed to in this way by a client. 'It would be great, they'd be so happy, you could spend time with the children.' But of course I can know none of these things. It might be awful, his in-laws might resent him, and the children might choose that week to be impossible!

Me: You suddenly felt trapped?

This appeared to be the most important statement to highlight, because it sounded so out of place with what he had said. 'Trapped' was a strong word to use in the circumstances of a family holiday, and was perhaps indicative of an important element in his relationship and in family life.

Liam: You know. Being at everyone's beck and call. Can't use the car, it's wanted to bring someone to the shops, to the doctor. Can't watch telly, there's a kid's programme on, or it's not suitable for kids. Can't do anything I want to. Always someone or something – talk, talk, talk. At times I feel my head will explode. And then I go to work and it's still talk, talk, but I can pretend to be busy, stocktaking or something, and spend time working at that. At home there's no escape, but always someone demanding things from me – money mostly – making noise and asking questions. Trapped inside my head.

Me: It sounds like you feel there's no escape, and I'm wondering if you feel that applies here too?

The use of the image of being trapped suggests that one would like to escape but there's no way out. I felt it was important that Liam stay with the trapped sensation, and experience it within this current situation, in the counselling session, where he is not in fact trapped but free to go at any moment.

Liam: At times I do feel I'd like to run away, but somehow knowing that I *can* means that I don't have to. It's like it's up to me, and that's OK.

This suggested that Liam was feeling some element of choice and decision around his counselling, because he appears to deal with his difficulties outside – including money – by closing his eyes and hoping they will go away. Alternatively *he* will go away.

Liam: But there's no rest at home and there isn't any escape, is there? I'm stuck there until hell freezes over.

An aunt of mine used to use that phrase, and I struggled to put her out of my head and stay with Liam in his unhappiness.

Liam: It was better before the kids came. Less commitment, less responsibility. We had more fun. There is an escape, but it seems so drastic. I could go to America or England. I've relatives there and would have no trouble getting a job. But I don't really want to leave Jean and the kids. They may drive me wild, but I don't want just to leave them. I'd miss them and it would be like running away, but maybe they'd all be better off without me. I suppose I want to eat my cake and have it. I want a way of staying and being more able to survive my family.

A long silence followed, while Liam surveyed his dilemma. He was beginning to look closer at himself, at his marriage and at his part in family relationships. At times he feels he'd like to walk out on the whole lot, leave the country, disappear, but he also at times clearly stated his wish to stay. He is beginning to acknowledge how difficult and painful life is for him within the family. Having shared so much, he spent the rest of the session telling me about his children, stories that demanded no deep thought or emotional experience. It was if he felt he had looked deeply into himself and his life, and wanted to tread water for a while, to regain his composure. We ended with relief on his part, agreeing to meet in three weeks time.

Session 12

Liam came to this twelfth session depressed and flat. I must confess I had hoped that the time down the country would have gone well, been enjoyable, and that Liam would begin to fit in better with his wife's family. My heart sank at his very first sentence!

Liam: I went to the birthday party down the country, and it was just as bad as it could have been. Everyone playing happy families and the whole thing totally unreal. The kids enjoyed it, and I really tried hard. Jean becomes another person when she's there, like a small child again. She really fits in, but tries too hard to please the folks, ordering me around to do messages, and belittling me in front of everyone there. I tell you I came close to blowing up!

Me: You really felt close to blowing your top.

Liam: All the talk was about the good old days, and people and relations I'd never heard of. And when I asked, at the beginning, it was a case of 'Oh you know. Don't be stupid, tiresome, thick – you've heard me mention him before.' And maybe I did, but then there's so many of them. I can't keep up, and I don't want to keep up. (His voice rose.)

Me: You were really angry with them all.

Although Liam sounded angry when he spoke of all the members of his wife's family, he backed away from the rage. There was a wistful note when he mentioned his own lack of extended family. Relating to his wife while in her family circle changes their relationship, as he has little experience of having his own role within this close community.

Liam: I suppose I'm used to just myself and my sister. We didn't have any cousins in Ireland – and few enough anywhere else. I think there were rows or divisions some time. My parents didn't and wouldn't talk about their families. And it's too late now. My father died when I was twenty-two, and my mother is gone very forgetful.

Me: You find this large and busy family very hard to cope with?

Liam: My parents were private people. We kept to ourselves. The worst thing we could do was talk outside about something at home. It made it very hard at school. I remember once the factory in the next town where my father worked was on short time, but he left as usual at 7.30 every day. And I said something to my best friend at school, and it got all around. There was trouble then I tell you. I was about seven or eight. The gang used to ask me questions just because they knew I wouldn't answer, or I'd make something up. And they went on and on, and jeered and laughed.

Me: It sounds very cruel and it must have been very tough on a small boy.

Liam: (With some surprise) I suppose it was – and now here I'm telling you all this and it doesn't seem to matter. Nobody will make me pay. I thought about running away a lot – but where to go? There was really no way out.

Me: Like the 'trapped' you mentioned earlier?

Liam: Yeah. God, I used to hate them all and I used to fight a lot. But they always won and I gave up in the end because I'd get belted at home for getting belted at school. No winning there, just keep the head down and wait – wait for what? I couldn't see any changes coming.

I got the sense that Liam had never really revisited his childhood. It had been closed off as an unhappy section of his life, and he seemed surprised to now see how difficult it had been. He also seemed to be completely unaware, as he spoke, of the connections that appeared so obvious to me as I listened to him: silenced, fearful, waiting, with the only apparent choice being to leave and go away.

Session 15

Liam continued to speak of his childhood, so much locked away for so long. Counsellors at times worry that much of their work consists of clients remembering their past, rather than dealing with the here and now, but we are living in the shadow of that past. To remain consistently and endlessly reflecting on what has gone before would obviously not be very productive, but if we can illuminate those dark places, we can gain some understanding of why today we are as we are. In this way the present becomes more manageable and more within our own choice, when we know 'why'. One picture in particular which Liam shared has stayed vividly with me.

Liam: My father drank heavily so money was always short. My mother used to stand at a window upstairs in the dark, looking down the street, watching for my father to come home on pay day – and sometimes he didn't come home at all. She used to talk endlessly and quietly as she stood there – on and on in a monotone. About how she knew I wouldn't be like that when I grew up, how cruel and unthinking my father was, what would we do now for money; no food, no heating, nothing. I used to think the only thing that would stop her was if she could die, and then I'd be free.

Me: Even remembering it is very painful.

Bills and money and even Jean seemed very far away, as we sat with the unhappy small boy torn between loyalties, between love and hatred, dreading the row which was coming. Liam was oblivious to me and to his surroundings, as he sat rigid in the misery which he had slipped back into, and I did not have to say anything. Finally he wept a little – harsh, painful tears – and just before he left, he said:

I used to wish I was somewhere else, anywhere else. So angry with Dad and yet he always came home singing, well away from the misery surrounding Mam, and he didn't really care. He didn't even bother having a row. This used to make her really mad.

During sessions 16 to 20, Liam spoke intermittently about leaving his relationship. He was obviously being pulled both ways. He talked and talked around the idea of 'escaping' from his life and his commitments, to such an extent that I wouldn't have been surprised if I had had a phone call from England saying he had left. He discussed how he could get work in London, friends he could stay with, and the freedom he would enjoy and whether it would be better to go further afield and cut totally from his old life. He came in to this twentieth session anxious and depressed.

Session 20

Liam: It's like when I was small, I used to be able to close it all out and be somewhere else. I used to just close her voice out and imagine being at the zoo or in China or anywhere, and it sometimes worked for a little while. And last night Jean and I had a particularly bad row about new clothes for the kids, and I suddenly wondered was I doing the same thing with her – imagining and wishing myself somewhere else, anywhere else.

It is always amazing, and very rewarding, when a client articulates something, makes some guess, that I have been wondering about for some sessions. I had come close to mentioning the similarity of his dealing with both mother and wife, the repeating of this pattern, and had hesitated lest Liam defensively dismiss it as nonsense. Now here it held validity because he had reached this conclusion for himself.

Session 25

Liam continued to make connections with himself as a small boy and began to recognise patterns put in place then and still in place today. He began to be aware that they may always be there, but that he need not be a prisoner within them. He recognises that for him money equals trouble, and is the source of tears and desperation, unhappiness and anger. He is finding some insight into himself and how he has been dealing with his wife as he dealt with his mother, as if she was the cause of his misery, and locking her out because she represents the voice worrying and nagging, and looking to him as the 'only hope' of rescue. I was aware that he was starting to look at strategies for change, and yet he surprised me with his next move.

Session 30

Liam: I asked Jean if we could do it differently. Perhaps we could take some time every week, even half an hour, to look at bills and so on, and she said OK. I was surprised at how pleased she seemed to be. The accounts guy in work has helped me to make a plan which is working so perhaps Jean can help with this. I still dream at times of getting away, but it's no longer running away. It's taking time for me, on my own. Or we may even get to the point where just the two of us could go away for a weekend, when Anthony gets older – let the in-laws earn their keep for a change!

Liam is no longer so bitter. He still doesn't like his in-laws, and possibly never will, but he is now able to say so and work around it, accepting this in himself.

Me: You feel if you could work together, then things wouldn't be so difficult. They mightn't be perfect, but you would be choosing how to deal with them.

Liam: I think it might work, because I really don't want to lose them all. During the good times I enjoy being a dad, and I think I can be a good one, and maybe we can make more good times. Perhaps if we give it a go, I can even enjoy being a husband more. If Jean and myself could talk more about what is happening, without fighting. I know we fight a lot, as if I'm blaming her for a lot, and maybe she's blaming me too. But I do love the kids. Here – (and he pulled out a photo of three small children to show me). I've been wanting to show you this for ages. You can see they're special.

Me: Yes, they are special, and I can see you're very proud of them.

And he literally shone with pride; I saw a different Liam to the unhappy man who came every week for help.

Session 35
Liam expressed his wish to end. He felt he had made progress, and could manage better for himself, especially with his wife's help. And of course, he said with a grin, he really couldn't afford to keep coming! What did I think? I told him I was glad to hear of the progress, and while I did feel there could be more work around his childhood and his new sense of self, and a longer time to consolidate his progress, he could of course come back at any time in the future if he felt he wanted to examine these pieces further. I asked if he would like to return for two further sessions, in order to look at where he was right now, survey the work he had done, and close our relationship, which had lasted for almost a year. He did so, and his mood was

both scared and hopeful for the future. I told him that I would miss our sessions, and I wished him well.

Endings of the counselling relationship are never easy, but I felt it was particularly important for Liam to face this ending and be fully present to its sadness, its finality, and his responsibility for the decision. He did discuss the fact that, hitherto, his way of ending relationships was to walk away, disappear, ignore the other person, and often finally feel rejected, as if they had dismissed him.

Thinking back over our sessions, I realised how much Liam's inner spirit had been damaged by his need to please others, to make it right for them, and the accompanying feeling of being burdened and trapped. He had lived his life according to what he perceived others wanted for him and from him, in order for them to love him. His need to be accepted by others, along with his very poor image of his self that he wished others would love, meant that when anyone did come close to him, he either pushed them away, or felt inclined to run away and disappear, lest they see the real Liam inside, which could never 'measure up'. There were so many secrets bottled up, so much hidden pain and loneliness, that it was actually surprising that he hadn't already cut and run from his marriage and family. His image of himself had been of someone who was totally inadequate, who failed every day at being husband, provider, father.

Liam had become more independent, less diminished by his inner critical voice and what others might say, and more his own real organismic self. He is beginning to move, at least in the direction of fulfilling his potential and of becoming more 'fully functioning'. Obviously there was no 'happy ever after' scenario, his bills are still pressing, money is always short, his in-laws are still not liked. His progress has been in his increased awareness of himself and how he relates to others. Once he began to accept himself as a person who would like to be these things, but who was not quite managing, and to recognise the reasons why this was so difficult, he began to be more accepting of himself and able to see beyond the image of himself that must shape up to the expectations of others. No longer wishing that he was an *ideal* husband and provider, he began to be a more real person, more mature, more self-accepting of his strengths and weaknesses.

And while I might have wished even more progress for him, and felt he would have benefited greatly from further sessions, I was also glad of the strides he had made.

Notes

1. Dave Mearns and Brian Thorne *Person-Centred Counselling in Action* (Sage, 1999) 163.

4

Listening

Listening, of this very special, active kind, is one of the most potent forces for change that I know.[1]

Importance of being understood
It may seem too obvious to mention, but listening is at the heart of all good relationships, including the counselling relationship. There are many forms of listening – distracted, hungry, surface, patient, listening to what is not being said, as well as listening to body language, tone, inflection, texture. It is so easy to allow our own concerns to distract us from the speaker. Am I preparing what I will say in response, guessing what will be said next, concentrated on my own state of being, focused on current feelings of sadness or anger within myself stirred before ever this person spoke to me? Am I merely offering secondary listening, concentrating on one element while carrying on with the other automatically? We need to deconstruct our listening, get to know and be aware of all the different elements in it in order to try and put all the pieces together seamlessly and listen totally, without distraction, our concentration entirely on the person who is speaking to us.

And while he is perhaps referring more to an inner personal music of natural sounds, John Burnside articulates something about the act of listening which chimes with my own attempt to hear what others are saying and feeling: 'I know that the real trick to being alive, the one worthwhile skill I might possibly learn in my cluttered life, is the art of listening: the art, in other words, of hearing not just the obvious, but that other, sparer, music concealed behind all the racket that we carry with us.'[2]

Sometimes an experience only becomes real, and therefore manageable, after we have related it, after it has been heard by another person. For example, after an operation, or violent event, we tell others how bad it was, blow by blow, over and over again. Perhaps the importance lies in the assembling of words and feelings, in the articulated sharing, in the feeling of not being alone in the experience any more, in the caring and (hopefully) the understanding of the other person. It lies in hearing ourselves make even partial or sequential sense of the senseless.

We constantly try to show others, especially those who are important in our lives, how life is for us – *exactly*. We fear above all not being understood, and being rejected in our efforts to share our experiences. We try to communicate just how we feel, precisely what we think. We make great efforts to encode and transmit our inner self and ideas, to win the space to accurately portray what it is like to be me. At the basis of all communication is this effort to describe what yesterday's sunset looked like, the precise point on the road where I fell off my bicycle, just exactly how angry I was with my colleagues.

Our difficulty is compounded when we consider the nature of language itself, and how poor a vehicle it often is for conveying any message, never mind a statement of deeply-felt emotions. 'When *I* use a word,... it means just what I choose it to mean – neither more nor less.'[3] Considering how difficult it is to achieve even an approximation of understanding, how impossible it is ever to be fully understood, it is little wonder that we expend such effort in our attempts. Our golden message, so clear and so obvious to us, is sabotaged first of all by our own inadequacies, our fears that no one will be interested, by blockages of language, or embarrassment, and secondly by the fact that our audience may be distracted, hard of hearing, unimaginative, tired or lazy – and ultimately perhaps only interested in their own selves! To add to this list of obstacles, what my client is telling are the facts from *her perspective*, and I listen from mine, and our inner pictures are, must be, totally different. We all know members from a family or group who describe an event, and although each person was there when it occurred, yet the memories and even the sequence of events are quite different. Remaining aware of difference, of response, of impact, of memory, helps me to accompany my client rather than direct her, to focus on her feelings rather than on my own, and to be more open to hearing beyond the words to her perceptions.

For vulnerable people only total understanding will suffice, an absolute which of course is not possible. Without this they can be disappointed, and defend themselves against being hurt by taking shelter in shyness, in avoidance, by becoming aggressive, even by falling ill. Expecting to be misunderstood, they can find it very difficult to accept that a listener is trying hard, and at least partially understands.

The subjective focus of our communication can make it very difficult, if not impossible, to know *exactly* what is meant, but in counselling, it is vital that I illustrate my tangible, visible effort to understand, and above all, that I never pretend understanding.

For many clients, it is their very inability to share their difficulties with others that has created the unhappiness that brings them to counselling. It is not surprising that a focused listener who is willing to try hard to understand, to be open about her efforts and seeking clarification when she is not understanding, being acceptant of whatever we disclose, can create an environment of safety rare in our experience, within which we can not only be heard, but can hear ourselves, the words we use, the ideas we create, the feelings that threaten us and our stability. Of course I cannot manufacture an instant two-way safety net within which to work, but I can provide the ingredients for the creation of such a relationship. These include boundaries of confidentiality, privacy, time, and my ability to embody the personal qualities that inspire and facilitate safety and trust. I can be accepting and non-judgemental, empathic and understanding, real and genuine in my purpose and openness, to a greater or lesser degree. Such listening is never an inactive reception of confidences and explanations. It remains vibrant, active, interested, and part of a process which is never inert.

Listening relationship

'Clients can overcome many problems on their own, but there are some individuals unable to overcome them on their own without assistance. It is then that they come to therapy.'[4] And indeed, many people have coped well all their lives and have now reached a life event which seems to defeat them, and they seek help with this.

Like other relationships, this counselling relationship moves through stages. The beginning is marked by uncertainty and the unknown on the part of both client and counsellor. The second stage moves towards a feeling of safety and familiarity, of

trust and acceptance, and the final stage of a successful counselling relationship is when the risky possibility of change is
faced and explored leading to a 'successful' outcome. This is an
ideal description, as the relationship often ends before I am
happy that the work is completed, as a result of outside circumstances or fear of the process on the part of the client. I
must also remember that my client's agenda may be directed
towards a very different outcome to that hoped for by me.

'I listen to "languages of the unsayable", those negations,
revisions, smokescreens and silences that mark what is unspoken and potentially unspeakable.'[5] Clients are sometimes hesitant about sharing their pain in therapy, reluctant to inflict their
unhappiness on us, the counsellors, with whom they have
formed a good relationship. They may fear that a trouble shared
would not be a trouble halved, but doubled. In the same way,
clients may not have spoken openly to partners, relatives or
friends. I believe it is important that I somehow convey my ability to listen to the story, allow it and explore it, without taking
on the burden of their unhappiness.

Clients also can be fearful that we are not *capable* of hearing
and accepting their story. Would we ask them to leave? Would
we refuse to believe them? Would we dismiss their story by saying, in effect, 'That's impossible! That couldn't have happened.'
We need not only to be strong enough in ourselves to hear and
receive their experiences, but also to convey to them somehow
in advance that we have this strength. We need to show that we
are both available and willing to hear them. Counsellors hear
harrowing stories, often prefaced with the words: 'I've never
told this to anyone before', and the telling is painful and distressing. The client may relive the experience in the counselling
session, and the counsellor needs to listen, to share and to survive, while hearing of cruelties beyond our experience, indigni-

ties and bullying and pain inflicted, all shared in the hope that the counsellor will absorb and survive them. At times clients lead up to horrors in small steps to see if we are willing and able to hear them. Neil Belton writes about Helen Bamber, the young woman who worked with victims of torture after World War II. She was not working as a counsellor, but she embodied many of the strengths of counselling work, as she listened to the survivors. She explained that 'You had to listen and to *receive*... and in that act of taking and showing you were available you were playing some useful role.'[6] She believed that 'you could listen people into telling their stories', and that you could encourage and make easier the telling. And if part of that telling was angry and resentful, we need to be able to absorb the angers, which may be directed at the counsellor as the only available target; 'And in her capacity to take their anger, she was showing a capacity to absorb without responding in kind, creating, however intermittently, an environment in which such feelings were safe.'[7] 'You don't do this work to be loved by the people you help. Sometimes the healthy thing for them is to attack you; and you have to be ready for that.'[8] (Of course, if the anger is correctly directed at the counsellor, for some real or imagined 'error', then this will need to be openly discussed and dealt with within the relationship.)

Careful, attentive listening enables the counsellor to hear the story and the words, and also to hear the gaps in the story, to note the parts which are skimmed over, to be aware of the almost palpable avoidance which a client may resort to rather than continue on a painful topic. We often hear a torrent of words which we sieve carefully in order to retain the vital clues to our client's inner self. Clients structure the truth – as we all do – and embroider the story as they tell it, and the counsellor is trying to absorb the meaning and the feelings present, rather than play detective by pointing out that last week the client said she was six years old when an event occurred, and now she says seven!

If it should become apparent that she is knowingly not telling the truth, I will try to accept that she has a reason for doing so, which I do not as yet know, and this reason may be an important part of why she is here, or how we will work together. She may be testing my willingness to believe her, or it may be what she believes I want to hear, or it may be the only 'truth' she can live with publicly right now. I may find an opportunity later on to explore this with her, or I may not. It is important to our relationship that I manage to remain accepting of her in her inability to be truthful. Listening to the glossed over and unsaid of the client's story contributes to a picture, however incomplete, of the hidden emotional world of the client. It can be like a jigsaw puzzle presented as a jumble of pieces, without a picture to follow, without tidy edge-pieces, where to join even two pieces can appear like a major achievement. Connections are achieved, but with much effort and even more patience. My client's sharing is often as much a sharing with themselves as with me as listener. She may need a 'witness' to make the unreal real, to render the unacceptable acceptable.

Listening to the unsaid

Mearns and Thorne point out that clients may be able to speak directly and clearly about issues that are not very difficult for them, but they 'typically have some themes or life situations that are much more fragile than others.' These will be alluded to indirectly and can very easily be missed by the counsellor, even one who prides herself on being a good listener. They will be expressed 'in side comments while leaving the session, or in themes buried within long stories, or by comments made very tentatively and then quickly denied.'[9] Such 'door-knob' comments may be slight, but may contain the key to a hitherto confusing impasse. It is as if the client knows that it is time to go, so a piece of information is offered, without any possibility of it being focused on right now, but also with the certainty that the issue has been flagged. The client trusts (and perhaps also fears) that the counsellor will have heard and will bring the topic back into focus in a later session, even if the client feels unable to introduce it again.

During our sessions, a client told her painful story while appearing from time to time to be on the verge of tears. At these moments she 'blanked'. For a few seconds she became completely still, her eyes became unfocused, and then she continued her story, as if on the other side of the pain. I shared with her what I was seeing and she said immediately: 'Oh yes. I've been told that I blank out at times', and carried on as if this were the most normal thing in the world. I became aware that this occurred every time the story came to a certain time in her life, but when I shared this insight, (which I thought was a good observation!) the client hotly denied any such connection. But the blanking didn't happen again, as if by bringing the connection into focus, it ceased to be necessary as an avoidance technique. It brought into her conscious awareness how she was skirting a painful place, and an awareness also that the counsellor had seen and accepted this avoidance. Although she was not prepared to admit just then what was happening, becoming conscious of her own avoidance enabled her to decide to stay with the painful experience, which she did in subsequent sessions.

'Rogers believed that a human being deserves the deepest respect for what he or she *is* no matter how worthless or inadequate he or she may *feel*.'[10] It is the work of the counsellor to allow experience and exploration of the worthless and inadequate feelings of the client while offering respect and acceptance and positive regard for the person. The hope is that eventually the client will come to an acceptance and respect for himself, and it will be readily seen that one of the main requirements is patience. Such change does not happen speedily. Rogers valued this quality of patience: 'Sometimes it seemed to me that this [patience] was the most valuable commodity we possessed: a willingness to wait through talk, silence, vituperation, ambiguity – a willingness to wait for the process to develop at its own pace.'[11]

We do listen to the stories and difficulties of our clients, but the client is never an object to be investigated, and curiosity is never the important element. This person is more than one part of a category of people. The very act of attentive listening can create for the client a sense of identity, of mattering, a feeling of reality, reflected by the counsellor who accepts the client as a real person in her own right. Addressing a group of people, a speaker welcomed them as 'teachers, nurses, or whatever', and surely would have been amazed at the level of annoyance in his audience of those who felt they were being dismissed as 'whatevers'!

In the same way, a client got quite angry with me, when I highlighted what I believed was a painful issue for him: 'This is more than an issue – this is *me*, and I am not an issue!' People need to feel that they really do matter, because counselling is not about solving problems, it is about helping people who have problems. When working with someone who is ill, I can at times feel as if the illness were sitting in a third chair, distracting me from the person of the client. I could make the mistake of filtering the story through the illness, and have merely an indistinct picture of the real person. My focus can be mistakenly on the illness, rather than on the person who is ill.

Listening well enables me to understand a current obstacle for my client, but it can be difficult to remember that the world and desires beyond that obstacle are unique to the client. What I *hear* may be only a reflection of what is important: accurate enough, but insubstantial, an echo of something deeper. Whatever image I may have of the outcome I would like for her, my client's picture is almost certain to be very different. This focused and attentive listening 'is indeed a most potent force for change, enabling a client to hear herself through the medium of the counsellor, recognising herself in the accurate reflection by the counsellor.'[12]

Listening to a situation with all our senses, observing and listening with our eyes as well as with our ears, can extend our awareness of others beyond their story as told, because sometimes clients do not have the facility with words that we imagine. In an old person's home, an elderly lady, restricted in movement and speech, would suddenly begin to struggle and fling off her clothes, in such a sudden and unexplainable way that it was believed she suffered from a kind of fit or seizure. Being perceived as a threat to herself, she was sedated much of the time. Although the patient had great difficulty in speaking, a new nurse persevered and eventually managed to understand that she suffered from episodes of becoming overheated, and unable to say how uncomfortable she was, she resorted instead to tearing at her clothes. The result of the new understanding was a reduction in her medication and a more consistently comfortable person, with more easily removeable clothes!

Responding

It is a fundamental tenet of person-centred counselling that 'our behaviour is to a large extent an acting-out of the way we actually feel about ourselves and the world we inhabit.'[13]

Merely telling our story, without sharing the accompanying feeling, is like a black and white movie, shorn of colour. The focus of Rogers on feelings came first of all from his belief that, when problems and difficulties were being focused on, our feelings were often not taken seriously into account, and were looked on as merely passing 'whims'. In moments when the individual discovers and connects with some feeling hitherto concealed from even himself, perhaps a deep fear beneath angry episodes, then 'the individual in such a moment, is coming to *be* what he *is*.'[14] Knowledge of our feelings as impetus to action and thought enables us to understand why we are thinking and behaving as we are, and how to change – if that is what we wish – yet so often, for so many people, this is the area most difficult to access, and to explore.

The willingness to acknowledge, explore and express our feelings results in the discarding of our masks, our false self-images, and allows us to be our real selves. 'When a person is living behind a front, a façade, his unexpressed feelings pile up to some explosion point, and are then apt to be triggered off by some specific incident.'[15] To others this explosion appears both unreasonable and inappropriate, but it may in reality be the final straw in a series of unacknowledged events. The damage such outbursts can do to a relationship needs no elaboration.

The charge has been levelled at Rogers that he focused too exclusively on feelings and not enough, if at all, on thinking and acts of will. On the contrary, for Rogers 'the human person was a unity where thinking, feeling and willing demanded parity of esteem.'[16] He has been criticised as anti-intellectual, a charge which often seems to spring from those with a dislike (or fear) of the expression of feelings. 'An approach which consciously goes about divesting the therapist of power and instead puts the control in the hands of the client is a monumental threat to all those therapists, whether men or women, who believe and want the power to help or to cure to be in their own hands and to be the result of their knowledge and expertise.'[17] Strong words!

Rogers explored subjective experience and far from being anti-intellectual, this is rather the combining of intelligent knowledge with feelings and experience – a unifying and inclusive construct. 'Once such a troubling feeling has been felt to its full depth and breadth, one can move on.'[18] Perhaps the 'anti-intellectual' label is used because PCA 'opens wide the doors to the expression of feelings and the experience of intimacy engendered by acceptance and understanding',[19] and many counsellors from other disciplines may not be comfortable with this way of working with clients.

Skills or techniques are helpful if they convey the core conditions or if they assist the client in exploration or clarification of confused statements or emotions. Eye contact conveys my attention; repeating a phrase from last week underlines my focus and enables my client to clarify her story; remaining silent at a time of emotional stress allows her to stay with and experience feelings which may have been denied to awareness until now. Silence enables reflective time, when my client can hear herself, can feel sad and stay with the sadness, can make a comment such as 'I'm a bad mother' and hear it and debate it within herself. In another context, the listener is likely to rush in to reassure, and the comment is put aside until the next time it surfaces, when it may once again be patted into obscurity. It is, however, important that silence be accepting, and companionable. For many clients, particularly at the start of the relationship, silence can be fearful and threatening. Their previous experience of silence has been punitive, especially in an unequal relationship such as parent and child, where silence may have become a symbol of misused power.

Expanding comments in an attempt to make previous statements clearer is also valuable, so long as it is offered tentatively, because while it may be correct and helpful, it may also be very wrong. For example, if my client appears to be struggling to share some event in her life, but is overcome with embarrassment as she finally blurts out whatever is causing her difficulty, I have a choice of response. Which I choose will arise from my knowledge of this client's background, how established is our relationship, which response I believe might be most helpful, but essentially I will accept her embarrassment and not become embarrassed myself.

Some learned responses appeal to the counsellor, not just as a formula of words, but as a way of saying something important. If the intention and the motive are client-centred, then it does not really matter how the admired statement is made, whether in a new formula or a more mundane selection of words. For example, when a client appealed strongly to me to tell her what to do, I answered: 'I am not in a position to tell you what to do, but if I were, what would you like me to say?' and she immediately told me. She knew what she wanted to do, but she had hoped that I would put it into words for her, and take ownership and perhaps responsibility for the decision. This method of not answering with a solution, but neither just passing the question back, allowed her to postulate what I 'might' say, but even more clearly illustrated what it was she wanted to do. This was a 'technique' that I may well use again, if this kind of request arises. A similar response, where a client sought permission from a student counsellor to say bitter words about her mother, was equally effective: 'It doesn't feel right giving you permission to say it, but I would like to hear whatever it is.'[20] It is essential that we choose responses of our own, that sit well with us, rather than adopting the ill-fitting repetition of someone else's formula.

These skills can be valued and practised, but it is essential that their use arises out of a spontaneous response to the client here and now. Rogers wrote: 'I am *not* trying to "reflect feelings". I am trying to determine whether my understanding of the client's inner world is correct.'[21] I must remain aware of my basic belief that it is the client's frame of reference that is paramount and that it is her inherent right to make her own decisions. Learned responses parrotted from a book are likely to be empty of reference to this client right now. If they have become part of the way I speak, of the way I communicate, then they can issue from me as part of my congruent self, responding to the need and urgency and immediacy of this client. If what I 'do' emanates from how I 'am', then the result will be genuine and real, and more likely to be effective.

'At any moment in a therapy the therapist is making a decision about what to pursue, how to think about what she is presented with ... to scrutinise her own responses to what is being said or not said, and so on.'[22]

It can be very tempting when sitting with a client and not knowing where to go or what to reply, to rescue myself from this uncertainty. At times I can be seized by an urgency to 'do' something, to reassure myself that I am having some impact, doing some good, being an effective counsellor. Perhaps my client is 'stuck' and I want to 'move her along,' and I could resort to retrieving a technical term or an aspect of theory and articulate it. Usually it sounds untimely, but it may comfort me or impress my client, and it may be difficult to see that it is a disengagement from the immediacy and demands of the relationship right now. I might say: 'It sounds like an introjection to me', or 'You may be using a defence mechanism', and the unfortunate, if impressed, client may not understand these terms, but may be aware on some level, that something profound has been offered, and may mumble agreement and try to divert to something less uncomfortable. This can also create a set of new expectations for a client who already feels she is failing to meet the expectations of important people in her life, and now feels she is failing *me* by not 'moving on', 'getting better.' Such reliance on an interpretation based on a theoretical assumption takes the power back into the therapist's hands, because the counsellor's focus has shifted from the reality of this client on to the (safer?) platform of a theory written in a book.

Theory and structure

'Theory is a structure which enables the therapist to be with the patient during the difficult and incomprehensible times ... it is the relational aspects of the therapy that are crucial – the endeavour of the therapist to reach the patient.'[23] Adherence to the beliefs of the person-centred approach does not result in a mechanical or robotic presentation of the core conditions to clients looking for help. *How* these beliefs are implemented, lived and shared depends on the personality of the counsellor, who is attempting to be her real self in this relationship, and whose style of communicating, and therefore her therapeutic style, may differ greatly from others. The place for exploring theory is in supervision or in my own reflective time, and not in distraction from my focus and concentration on my client as he is in that moment, in our connecting relationship. 'Theorising should inform practice but it should not dictate it.'[24] Speculation and discussion in the light of theory have a proper place in the work, but belong outside the session.

'Therapy should not be theory-driven but relationship-driven.'[25] If I confine myself to a list of 'acceptable', tried-and-tested, therapeutic responses and behaviours, not only am I confining my natural responses and not being truly congruent, but I am also in danger of failing to respond to the unique and immediate needs of each client. While my theoretical foundation is the same, based on my PCA beliefs and training, my actual responses can vary greatly. If I remain true to myself and open to the demands of different clients (always a delicate balance) then I have a better chance of being effective. 'The patients' views of helpful events in therapy are generally relational, often involving some act of the therapist that stretched outside the frame of therapy or some graphic example of the therapist's consistency and presence.'[26] However, it must be emphasised that this is in no way a licence for experimentation, or snatching at any device which sounded good in a book or lecture. The confidence to be such a naturally-responding counsellor is likely to be slight at the beginning of our work, and to increase as we gain experience. When we feel a growing security in our work, and in our ability to accept ourselves as a 'good enough' counsellor, then we will be more able to use those attributes of ours which constitute our uniqueness, as a person and as a therapist.

Person-centred counselling is at times accused of being mild and gentle when compared to other forms of therapy which are sometimes seen as more likely to 'cut to the chase' in order to facilitate action and results. This impression often arises from a scanty knowledge of the theory, along with the notion that 'confrontation' must always be forceful. If I do not in some way challenge my client, then our work may remain repetitive and unmoving, but challenging does not have to be confrontative. (I suspect that this distinction is lost on many PCA critics.) 'Challenging' can also take the form of highlighting a client's statement to compare it with a previously expressed opinion: 'Some time ago you said you had the perfect childhood, but there seems also to be some memory of conflict as you hear the echo of loud voices and rows?'; of offering back to a client something they have said so that they can really hear it: 'You've talked before of hating him, and how you'd like to kill him, but you say too that you love him?'; of acknowledging an expressed feeling in similar but different words: 'You said you're a bit annoyed, but I hear you as quite angry.' To call these responses 'confrontations' is not the best description, but they do have the effect of focusing the person on some contradiction in what they have said. 'Confrontation ... stimulates and presents dissonant elements to the self-concept but in a way which is not experienced as threatening.'[27]

The challenge often comes from the client herself, when she hears what she is really saying, either from the words spoken by herself, or from the same words repeated by the counsellor. A client who told me about what she had been doing every week, invariably made little of her actions: 'I did fairly well', 'I felt I had done quite a good job', 'I suppose I like him quite well'. She looked on herself as a decisive person, and was almost incredulous when I said: 'I'm not sure are you aware of how you subtract from your achievements. Everything is 'quite' or 'fairly'. She started to listen to herself and quickly realised that it was so. She began to practice being more decisive in her words, and became more confident in herself. This is a minor example of how a small pointer worked as a challenging statement towards change. At a later stage in the relationship clients may become aware of our challenges and find them both effective and entertaining. A client once said: 'I was appalled to hear my sister spoken to in that way, and I was saying "ouch" to myself.' Aware of this person's inability to stand up for herself at painful times, the counsellor said 'Do you ever say "ouch" for yourself?'

Client: No. I cannot.

Counsellor: But you were very hurt at that remark to your sister?

Client: (with a laugh) Now I hear you saying 'ouch' for me!

There is always the dangerous possibility that our sessions could become comfortable, merely the telling of a story. 'Cushy' and 'cosy' are adjectives that do not belong in the counselling relationship! It can be hard sometimes to remember that therapeutic work continues between sessions. My client does not just close down for a week (though some clients try to do so) and come back and open the box again. During that week she will have reflected on our work, considered what was said, and often come to new awareness as a result. I can only see her within our relationship, but she has a life independent of me, filled with the busyness of living.

Impact on the counsellor
This special and deep relationship obviously has an effect on the counsellor also, and it is considered most important that counsellors in training be in some form of personal therapy themselves. This has the advantage, not only of giving them an appreciation of what it is like to be a client, but also of giving them scope to be more fully aware of their own selves and their process of becoming a fully-functioning person. Being in personal therapy also provides a safe place for the counsellor who is in contact with clients who may resonate uncomfortably with his own material, or threaten him in some perhaps not obvious way. Counsellors who have many years of experience also benefit at times from reconnecting with the experience of being a client, as a way of 'refreshing' their inner selves or providing a

resource when they experience either work-related or personal difficulties. Counsellors are required to be in on-going supervision while they are working, and these built-in protections or 'shock-absorbers' are a result of the general acknowledgement that the work has impact on the counsellor as well as on the client. It can be interesting at times to see how the inclusion of a supervisory opinion can alter the perceptions of the counsellor, and influence his way of working.

In this way, for example, if a romantic or sexual element appears to be present in the counselling relationship this will need to be openly acknowledged and addressed, first in supervision, and then, if necessary, with the client. (The ethical guidelines of the IACP and the other professional bodies address this possibility.) More usually the intimacy of the sessions is of a different nature, more of closeness at soul level, where the counsellor is open and trusting, without guile or need for control, without flirtation or defensiveness, and the client responds accordingly. Supervision can also focus on different elements within the relationship, which otherwise might not be obvious to the counsellor. For example, if dislike or exaggerated liking develops, it might prove beneficial to the relationship, and to the client's sense of safety, if this were addressed within the sessions, preferably as soon as the counsellor becomes aware of it. This is never an easy task, requiring openness and tact and no little risk.

At the end of a long counselling relationship, a client said to her male therapist: 'I haven't become romantically attached, but this has been perhaps the closest and deepest relationship I've ever had – as if we have been attached through both our heads and our hearts – but not romantically. It is very strange to look back on.' This acknowledgement that the relationship had been both unique and apparently therapeutic understandably pleased the counsellor. He was glad for the client and the work she had done, satisfied with his own part in her growth, but underneath he was aware of some small personal disappointment for himself. As a man he was somewhat disappointed that he had not impacted in some romantic way on this woman he had met and spent much time with. The work and the relationship had been as he had hoped it would be, but some masculine echo of pride felt let down because he had had no romantic impact![28]

These are the kind of small shadows we need to be continually aware of, so that we can be more fully aware of ourselves and of our potential impact on others. If this counsellor had not become aware of his disappointment, and been courageous enough to name it for himself, then he might have dealt differently with his next attractive client, perhaps even indulging in some male preening in an unconscious effort to, this time, impress her 'romantically'.

Theory then works alongside humanity in the person-centred approach. In the final analysis 'it is not the behaviour of the therapist which is important but the impact upon the client.'[29] My focus needs to be my client, and the impact of the work on her, without ever losing sight of its impact also on me. 'At its core, the therapeutic relationship remains an intensely human, personal, and essentially unique encounter.'[30] Rogers focused on the 'ordinariness' of the relationship, where someone in difficulty comes to another for help. No mystique, no potions, no magic spells, just the focus firmly on the client and their inner world and resources. Their difficulties can be relatively straightforward or they can be deep-seated and intransigent, requiring a longer period of time. 'Therapy is a set of processes that simply build on and enhance clients' own naturally occurring self-righting processes ... As people dialogue they are changed.'[31]

The idea of self-righting is very graphic, giving a picture of a comparatively stable individual, living life on a fairly even keel, meeting an unexpected obstacle, floundering for a time, and then finding their way back to equilibrium.

'All I could do was sit and listen.' If we could only fully appreciate what a valuable act of giving this is, we would use this plaintive phrase less often, and perhaps even become boastful: 'There wasn't much anyone could do, but I was able to listen!'

Notes

1. Howard Kirschenbaum and Valerie Land Henderson, eds., *The Carl Rogers Reader* (Constable, 1990) 136.
2. John Burnside, 'A moment in the midnight sun' in the *Irish Times Magazine* 5 Jan 2002, 66.
3. *Through the Looking Glass* Lewis Carroll (1872) (The Bodley Head, 1974) 197.
4. Karen Tallman and Arthur C. Bohart 'The Client as a Common Factor' in *The Heart and Soul of Change* Mark A. Hubble, Barry L. Duncan, Scott D. Miller, eds., (American Psychological Association, 1999) 120.
5. Annie G. Rogers (interview with John Broderick) *Eisteach, Vol. 2 No. 20* (Spring 2002) 34.
6. Neil Belton *The Good Listener* (Weidenfeld and Nicholson, 1998) (Phoenix 1999) 109.
7. Ibid., 161.
8. Ibid., 379.
9. Dave Mearns and Brian Thorne *Person-Centred Therapy Today* (Sage, 2000) 154.
10. Brian Thorne *Carl Rogers* (Sage, 1992) 45.
11. Kirschenbaum and Land Henderson *The Carl Rogers Reader* 483.
12. Ursula O'Farrell *Courage to Change* (Veritas, 1999) 70.
13. Dave Mearns and Brian Thorne *Person-Centred Counselling in Action* (Sage, 1999) 7.
14. Carl Rogers *On Becoming a Person* (Constable, 1961) 113.

15. Ibid., 318.
16. Mearns and Thorne *Person-Centred Therapy Today* 76.
17. Ibid., 78-9.
18. Kirschenbaum and Land Henderson *The Carl Rogers Reader* 151.
19. Mearns and Thorne *Person-Centred Therapy Today* 75.
20. Personal statement to author.
21. Kirschenbaum and Land Henderson *The Carl Rogers Reader* 128.
22. Susie Orbach *The Impossibility of Sex* (Penguin, 1999) 72.
23. Ibid., 188.
24. Paul Wilkins *Person-Centred Therapy in Focus* (Sage, 2003) 40.
25. Irvin D. Yalom *The Gift of Therapy* (Piatkus, 2002) xviii.
26. Ibid., 37.
27. Dave Mearns Developing *Person-Centred Counselling* (Sage, 1994) 93.
28. Personal statement to author.
29. Mearns and Thorne *Person-Centred Therapy Today* 194.
30. Mark A. Hubble, Barry L. Duncan & Scott D. Miller, eds., *The Heart and Soul of Change* (American Psychological Association, 1999) 163.
31. Ibid., 120-1.

5

Siobhán

'I can't forget what I cannot remember.
And the jigsaw is not completed yet'.[1]

Siobhán
I have become aware over the years that listening well is more
than merely concentrating on what my client chooses to tell
me, and adding the facts together to reach a tidy sum of
knowledge. I am listening to what my client says, but in
addition I am trying to listen on different levels, trying to
remain aware of body language, inflection, tone, what is not
said, my own reaction to the story. And I have always found
it most difficult to listen to and take heed of myself, what is
happening within me as I sit with my clients, what are my
feelings and my ideas, for without this third listening ear, I
may miss important clues about my client. This is an account
of a client who taught me this lesson and who has remained
indelibly pictured in my head, and in my heart.

Siobhán, a beautiful and charming girl, came for
counselling some years ago because she wished that her life
could be different, and that she herself could be different. She
spoke freely and shared information about her secretarial job,

and her family. Aged twenty-six, she lived at home with her mother and three younger siblings.

Siobhán appeared somewhat shy, but as the weeks progressed, she seemed to be comfortable in the sessions. She had many acquaintances, but said she had no close friends and she would like to change this. She had been 'friendly' with several young men, but mostly met them in groups. She had had only a few 'dates' and some brief relationships which had been 'unsatisfactory'.

Session 5

Me: You mentioned last week that you'd like to be different and I'm not sure what you meant?

Siobhán: You know – different. More interesting, more to say.

Me: You don't feel you are interesting?

Siobhán: God no! I feel sometimes like a dead hand descending on a group – when I arrive and say something, it falls flat – no matter how much I'd rehearsed it, it comes out wrong and no-one answers me or takes much notice. I feel a fool.

Me: You find yourself rehearsing what you'd like to say.

Siobhán: Yeah – the way we all do. (Pause) Don't we?

There was silence for a few moments and I sensed the uncertainty in Siobhán as she weighed this – and then she was gone, moved on.

Siobhán: Anyway, I was at this party the other night ...

And she launched into a lengthy description of the party. The clear message I heard was that neither uncertainty nor any other feeling was going to be explored today!

Session 10

By session 10, I felt I knew a lot *about* Siobhán, but very little of the real person. I could not fathom why she had come for counselling. On the face of it, she was bright and popular, and she didn't seem to be able to get to any clearer description or understanding of what she meant by wanting to be different. We skated safely on the surface of her life and the only certainty I had was that she was adept at avoiding and deflecting any emotional exploration. At times I was bored, at times I felt powerless, and overall I had a sense of wasting time.

At the end of session 10, Siobhán asked me for direct feed-back.

Siobhán: How do you think I'm doing ?

Me: We've certainly discussed many of the important aspects of your life, but I have some sense that we're still on the surface.

Siobhán: Oh not really. I think you're doing a great job.

She had chosen to hear my concern for her in the work as rather a feeling that I was unsure and needed reassurance, which she duly gave me! I tried again:

Me: I don't have a clear picture of why you're here. It feels as if you are showing me a picture, but carefully not letting me any further in.

Siobhán: That sounds right, but I'm not sure what you want.

Me: It's not that I want anything, but you mentioned a few weeks ago that at times you would like 'to end it all, there was no point in continuing', and that sounded very important to me, but you haven't mentioned it again. Perhaps you'd like to come back to that but find it too difficult?

Siobhán: Not at all. It just doesn't seem the right time to discuss it now. I want to tell you about the holiday my friend Sarah is planning, and she wants me to go with her.

I registered inwardly 'Good! Holidays are good' and then wondered was I trying to reassure myself. She sounded so detached and matter of fact about so enormous a topic as suicide. Or had she been talking about ending the counselling sessions? What was I missing? Who had the key? Of course the client had, but nonetheless I searched desperately for it.

Sessions 10-17
Week after week Siobhán brought in a neatly packaged 'happening' – a row at work, a hurtful remark by a friend, a sharp comment by her mother – and safely discussed each one as if she were compiling a short thesis. Each story had a beginning, a middle, a reference point and a satisfactory conclusion at the end of each session.

Session 11

Siobhán: I had a row at work yesterday. My boss was in a bad mood and we all know to stay out of her way at such times. (There followed a long description of who said what to whom, how upset she was and what she did. It was like watching a film, because her ability to tell a story was very good.)

Me: I'm not sure what you mean by upset?

Siobhán: You know. Frightened.

Me: I'm aware that you hate people fighting, so this must have been hard for you, in the middle of your office. It sounds like you were caught in the middle.

Siobhán: Yeah. I tried to make a joke but it didn't work, so I went off to lunch.

And Siobhán remained insubstantial, like a shadow in a mirror. There was something skewed about the row, her fear, and going off to lunch. The pieces just didn't fit, but this is how she was presenting them. I learned about her household, her hobbies, her exercises, her school life and eventually her model childhood. She spoke of her relationships with her mother and her brothers, which seemed on the surface to be reasonable, neither perfect nor abysmal. Her father had died when she was sixteen, but he too was mentioned in a dispassionate way.

Session 12

In this session, Siobhán told me at length about her love of animals, and how she had hoped to be a vet. When her father had died ten years previously, she had had to opt instead for secretarial training, which cost less and offered the prospect of earning money sooner.

Siobhán: It's quite soulless really. You cannot interact with a machine on any real level! I remember being quite angry with my father for dying before we were all trained, as if he hadn't been a good enough provider. But I've made good friends at work and I quite enjoy the office I'm in now, so perhaps it was just as well.

If I had listened more closely, would I have heard more clearly this mention of anger towards her father for dying? I was concentrating on her career choice, and her disappointment about not becoming a vet, and did not register the incongruity of her expression of annoyance because her father had died without paying for her education, without showing any glimmer of sadness or loss.

Me: And yet you miss not being involved with animals?

Siobhán: I used to rescue injured birds and kittens and mind them. They always seemed so responsive and never demanded more than I had to give. I did my best for them and then they either got better or they died.

This was quite dispassionately said, although she seemed to have been really concerned for these sick creatures. The rest of the session was filled with stories of various adventures and bird and animal 'funerals', and her attempts to 'home' some of the strays.

Session 17

Siobhán mentioned that she had been visiting a friend in hospital during the week, and how it reminded her of being in hospital for some weeks when she was ten years old.

Siobhán: I had a skin condition, really bad, that wouldn't clear up, so they needed me in to cream me all over a few times a day. My mother wasn't very good at that kind of thing, and the boys were all small then, and needed lots of minding.

I was alert here for several possible threads: attention focused on small boys rather than on sick Siobhán; mother perhaps overpowered by her young family and not managing very well; the misery and pain of being separated from home for some weeks. But as usual, Siobhán surprised me.

Siobhán: I really had a ball – I loved every day of it. We had lessons and toys, and I don't remember any of the other children being very sick. The nurses were great fun and the doctors only appeared once a day. There *was* one I didn't like, he was very tall and he wore glasses, and he was quite scary.

I think I was so distracted by hearing that her hospital experience had been so enjoyable, the exact opposite of what I expected to hear about perceived abandonment and fear and strangeness, that I failed to pick up on the implicit message that hospital was better (safer?) than home. As for not exploring the one 'scary' element in the form of the tall doctor, it seems so obvious today that I find it hard to believe that I did not follow this through with a question like: 'He has really stayed in your mind. Was it because he was so tall or did he look like anyone you knew?'

Session 21
Siobhán had been to a concert and a following all-night party in a friend's house. Just before the session ended, she told me what had happened with one of the group.

Siobhán: This guy I quite fancy was messing around and we'd had a lot to drink. I couldn't bear his fumbling and told him to 'eff off', but he persisted so I hit him quite hard with a bottle. I don't know which of us was more surprised. Imagine, I hit him with a bottle and cut his head!

She sounded proud of her reaction, but also there were tears in the back of her voice.

Siobhán: I don't suppose he'll ever talk to me again.

Me: And you'd miss him if he disappears?

I had responded to the threatening tears and Siobhán wept briefly and told me she really liked him. She hadn't allowed tears before, and our time was up, so I postponed any elaboration of the 'messing around' and the 'fumbling'. Again in hindsight, perhaps it would have been more appropriate to at least mention these two phrases, if only to indicate that I had heard them and would be willing to listen further with her. She had not been so emotional in the sessions before, so I was aware that this had been an important sharing.

Sessions 22 to 30

Any attempt I made to refer back to session 21 was firmly stymied by Siobhán in the sessions that followed. Either she said she didn't want to 'go there', or she filled the sessions with talk of possible promotion at work, or she sat in silence. Any oblique reminders I made were totally ignored. I was so aware of how easily a client's story and memories can be 'contaminated' by an over-eager counsellor that I veered away when I found her unresponsive. The delicate balance between focusing on a particular part of the story, and respecting the client's wish or need to avoid or postpone staying with an important experience, held me off for many sessions.

At the same time I was aware that her overall mood was more depressive. She appeared to have little energy, and her repeated phrase 'What's the point?' began to wear me down. I felt myself almost sinking with her, and began to dread our sessions. Siobhán missed a couple of appointments, which she had never done before, and appeared to have withdrawn even from the surface relationship we had had. When her appearance and her grooming started to deteriorate, I became seriously worried. I fretted in supervision, and began to blame myself, and to look for help and solutions from my supervisor. Finally he asked me to concentrate on what was happening within me, and I realised that I was listening to Siobhán only and not to myself. As I shifted this focus in supervision, I became aware that for the last several sessions, I had had a recurring image of being in a dark room, warm and stuffy, where a butterfly beat its wings against a small window. I had dimly associated this with my own frustration, and dismissed it time and again. In session 31, I took a risk and trusted my own inner picture and the relationship which had developed between us.

Me: Siobhán, there's something I'd like to share with you, an image I have. It may be entirely my own and little to do with you, but it may also be important. If it has no resonance for you, please try to ignore it.

And I shared with her a brief outline of my butterfly image.

There followed a silence of at least ten minutes, during which time I inwardly berated myself for a fool, for being irresponsible, for all manner of foolishness. Siobhan's face remained blank as she looked at the carpet, but there was a tenseness and a stillness about her which was not natural, and which did not brook interruption. Finally, and painfully, as if each word were being slowly extracted, she said in a whisper:

Siobhán: How did you know? I cannot stay there, I cannot let it in. It's too dangerous.

And she began to shake all over, like a small child terrified by the possibility of monsters. The temptation to hug her and hold her was very great, but she did not need to be touched in that moment. I waited with her as she permitted me to see, and herself to experience a little of some great terror, and after a further ten minutes, during which she was silent, she collected herself and left, even though our session was not finished.

Siobhán did not turn up for her next session and sent no word, and I was left to go over and over what I had said, and to trust – and hope – that she, and our relationship, was strong enough to survive her near disclosure.

Session 32

Siobhán came in and sat down, with no mention of the missed session, and in a detached manner began to describe the horror of the abuse she had suffered from her father as a child, always in the same attic room in her house using 'the language of the unsayable and the unspeakable'. And she wept, as if she would never be able to stop, but when our time was up, she composed herself and left.

If I had become aware of my image, and shared it, earlier, would we have progressed more quickly? I will never know would she have come to that point in her own time, if I had not shared my picture. I took a risk and it worked, but not all such risks do work. Often they can be dismissed out of hand and we can feel a fool. I find I don't mind feeling like a fool if my reasons for sharing in this manner are an effort to help my client to clarify or mention an important experience – and never merely showing off my own imaginative leap! In this case I cannot be sure that my reasons for sharing were not more of a reflection of how difficult I found it to sit with Siobhán in her despair, rather than a strong sense of her hidden fear. However, I know I felt she was slipping out of the relationship, perhaps never to come back, and an opportunity to speak would be lost, perhaps never to present itself again. Above all was the strength of the image, and the sure knowledge that it did not originate within me.

Sessions 33 to 57
Siobhán's ability to switch her feelings on and off was less noticeable during the weeks that followed. She shared the details and surprised herself by being able to recall so much. Retrieving the memories and the impact of her father's abuse, she allowed herself to suffer and re-live much of the torment, but was able to close down and re-enter her current world when the sessions ended. She was still very controlled, but that control had served her well up to now. She was able to accept that this had happened

to her, that it was a part of her that no longer needed to be kept hidden in the dark recesses of her mind. Her reaction to the abuse had been one of completely splitting off the reality of the horror, and trying to live a carefully constructed 'ordinary' life. She had closed off the conflict between her love for her father and her hatred of his dealings with her, and it was when that concealment (even from herself?) was shaken by her wish for relationships with young men that she came looking for help. She had shut down her emotional and her sexual self so effectively that she found herself isolated and rejecting of her peers, and this tipped a balance in favour of finally acknowledging her past.

After fifty-four sessions, Siobhán told me she was planning to travel with a group of friends to Australia for a year, and that she would be ending counselling. We spent three sessions exploring what it would be like to end our relationship, and discussing and recalling our work together. I hoped that she felt happy with her decision to end, and that it was not merely a decision taken because she was going away, and she thought it was partly that, but also that a season of her life had ended, and she might re-connect later if she found she needed it. I was sorry to see her go, and glad to see that she felt able to go.

I saw Siobhán in town with a young man, two years later. She saw me too and visibly flinched and her eyes flickered away. We passed without acknowledgement as I feel strongly it is the client's choice whether to greet me or not. Perhaps I would have been too difficult to explain to her friend if we had stopped to say hello, perhaps I constituted too painful a connection, or perhaps she was merely 'caught on the hop'. I really had only one question: was she happy with how her life had progressed, and was she less haunted? And of course I will never know. The memory of her abuse will never leave her, but I do hope that it is no longer controlling her.

I remember a client who once came to me for help to assist him in facing his fear of exams. He had avoided or failed many exams in his life, and with his university finals approaching, he needed to be better able not to panic. We worked together for some months, and he left believing that he was in a better position to at least understand his fears. About five years later, I read in the paper about his achievements in his chosen profession, and felt very proud of my involvement in his success. More usually, the counselling relationship is like the middle chapter of a book, the ending of which we will never get to know. We enter our clients' lives, interact for a while, and then exit. So many unfinished stories!

And Siobhán is also like a single snapshot, with the follow-up pictures unknown to me. I feel I listened well to her story, but so much was hidden and muffled that for a long time, my picture was one-dimensional. Would I work differently if she were to come today? I do look back and wish I done this or this, and wonder would the result have been different, quicker, more in depth, if I had been more aware of the clues or lack of them? And there are no answers. I have learned from our relationship, however, because I am aware now that it was only when I recognised the shadow her pain cast on my own inner self, that I was able to access that pain, and afford her a connection between it and those around her. I had perhaps 'listened her into words'.

Notes

1. Constance Nightingale *Journey of a Survivor and other Poems* (Self-published, 1986) 8.

6

Core Conditions

'We are deeply helpful only when we relate as persons, when we risk ourselves as persons in the relationship, when we experience the other as a person in his own right.'[1]

Relationship
How do we attempt to create – and foster – this ideal and unique relationship? At the outset it is essential to remember that, in this imperfect world, we are always *aiming* to create the ideal, without ever fully reaching it. Through intensive recording and analysis of therapeutic sessions, Rogers isolated three characteristics of the counsellor which appeared to be most effective in creating the atmosphere of safety and trust within which the client could explore her unhappiness.

'On the basis of research findings, three attitudes or conditions appear to be most important for the success of therapy. They are:

1. the therapist's genuineness or congruence,
2. the therapist's complete acceptance or unconditional positive regard for the client,
3. the therapist's sensitive and accurately empathic understanding of the client's feelings and personal meanings.

Therapy appears to be maximally effective when all three are present in high degree.'[2] People other than clients who met Rogers during his life also appeared to experience these qualities. They said that 'he made them feel, not important, but accepted. He saw them and did not judge them. He didn't just hear what people said but he heard *them*.'[3]

These qualities enhance any relationship, but are perhaps more visible, and certainly more essential, in the therapeutic relationship, which after all 'can be a microcosm of how the client experiences their world.'[4] They are connected and overlapping, and it is difficult to imagine one on its own, as each shades into the others. Of the three, genuineness is believed to be the most important, and the most difficult to achieve. The core conditions foster relationship, maintain equality, create safety, offer unconditional acceptance.

Many therapists who work within different traditions subscribe to the usefulness of the core conditions in establishing the therapeutic relationship, which is acknowledged almost universally as being of prime importance in the work. Once the therapeutic relationship is established, however, they begin to employ those aspects of their particular theoretical stance which they believe applicable. The person-centred approach in contrast maintains that the relationship *is* the counselling because within that relationship, the client will be able to gain self-knowledge and make a choice towards change. 'In the person-centred approach there is no withdrawal from the relationship and retreat into exercises, interpretation or analysis of the client's behaviour. The relationship is *all*-important.'[5]

However it is not so clear that all three conditions are accepted equally by those working with different theories: 'the concept of congruence, with its emphasis on therapist genuineness and the relinquishing of professional power, has received a cool reception in most other therapeutic quarters.'[6]

At times Rogers could be quite scathing in defence of his own ideas, and his determination that the only expert present in the work was the client as expert in his own self. It is possible to imagine the impact his writings must have had on hitherto unchallenged practitioners in the area of psychology and related fields who were perhaps more accustomed to focus on the laws of behaviour and behavioural change, rather than on the subjective accounts and feeling states of their 'patients'.

'It is the client who knows what hurts, what directions to go, what problems are crucial, what problems have been deeply buried. It began to occur to me that unless I had a need to demonstrate my own cleverness and learning, I would do better to rely on the client for the direction of movement in the process.'[7] Believing this, I can also accept that the core conditions are not only necessary, but are also sufficient, for the client's work to progress. Unfortunately, it is often assumed that this is too simple a statement, and there is little realisation that the application of the core conditions is demanding and difficult in the extreme. The therapeutic relationship is perceived differently by the counsellor and by the client. I see it as *equal* at a level of humanness, with both persons being equally deserving of respect. The work is focused on the present meeting point between client and counsellor, and while it may not be a fully reciprocal relationship, there is equality present in the outlook and approach of the counsellor.

CONGRUENCE

'I believe it is the *realness* of the therapist in the relationship which is the most important element. It is when the therapist is natural and spontaneous that he seems to be most effective.'[8]

There is nothing ambiguous about this statement. It clearly points up the importance and centrality of congruence to Rogers' whole work, where the focus is on how the counsellor *is* in the session rather than on what she is doing, 'and as such it usually goes on unnoticed.'[9] If we are accustomed to speaking and acting from behind masks or disguises, then the laying aside of these can require courage and honesty, with perhaps an unfamiliar exposure and feeling of risk-taking. Such realness sounds attainable, but is difficult to achieve. It demands that the counsellor is constantly aware of her own inner feelings and sensations, including those in response to her client at any given moment. This awareness, and willingness to speak openly and truthfully from these reactions, if considered appropriate, shows us to be real, without mask or guile.

Rogers also used the terms genuineness, authenticity, and perhaps it is easier to grasp what congruence entails when we become aware of its absence. 'You don't know where you stand with her', 'I feel I don't know her at all', 'He never says what he means'. How congruent and real we are able to be will influence all our relationships. If I am not willing in my interactions with others to share much of myself, if I am not even aware of my inner feelings and reactions, then I may be presenting a picture of myself as someone who is more attractive, clever, helpful than I really am, and may be experienced as false and insincere.

Awareness of my feelings

Congruence, therefore, is a willingness to be open, to be truly oneself, to be seen to be, and experienced as, transparent. The congruent counsellor does not seek to give a picture of an expert, with ready answers and instant solutions. It is *not* merely self-disclosure, though at times this can result from being congruent.

It is important that I be aware of my feelings and reactions towards the client. If I am irritated by a client, and remain unaware of this irritation, then the way I communicate with him is likely to reflect this, at least in part, perhaps through a sharper tone, an impatient movement of hands or head. I may be speaking acceptant words, but, even without my knowing it, transmitting impatience. If I can remain aware of what is occurring within me, then I am less likely to give these contradictory signals or messages.

'Being genuine also involves the willingness to be and to express, in my words and behaviour, the various feelings and attitudes which exist in me.'[10] The important word here, which is often ignored, is 'willingness'. There is a great difference between 'expressing my feelings' and 'being willing to express my feelings'. When to communicate these feelings congruently is a difficult question, and one subject to ongoing debate and (often heated!) discussion. Obviously to express all I am feeling would not be possible. The client would not get a word in edgeways! I believe we need to trust ourselves sufficiently in the work to 'call' the decision whether or not to share of ourselves in the moment, to allow ourselves to take the risk. Like all such instant decisions, we may be wrong, and in some cases we may be very wrong. There is no overall rule to follow, merely our immediate estimate of what will best serve the client's needs and how to phrase the resulting response.

Mearns and Thorne[11] offer three guidelines for such moments. They believe that congruence is expressed as 'the counsellor's *response* to the client's experiencing.' The counsellor's flow of feelings within her are not all for expression, but only those which are *relevant* to the immediate concern of the client, and those which are '*persistent* or particularly *strik-*

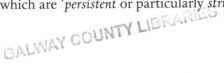

ing'. There is obviously no room here for the counsellor to merely blurt out whatever she feels is within her at any given time.

However, it is important that what I *do* say reflects or matches what I am feeling at that given moment. This may not be easy, but can have very positive results. A counsellor working with a somewhat repetitive client, found herself on a sunny afternoon after lunch sitting with her, struggling to remain awake. She heard the client say: 'I think you're falling asleep on me', and where many of us might have jerked upright hotly denying any such possibility, the counsellor answered, 'Do you know, you're right. I find it very warm and heavy here today. Perhaps I might open a window.' But the client concurred, 'I'm finding it very heavy myself. It's a real burden and I don't know how I'm going to manage', and she moved unthinkingly into a part of her story which up to now had been described as 'a piece of cake' and 'no bother'. Somehow the fact that the counsellor didn't try to deny her sleepiness allowed the client to cease avoiding her own difficulty.

A somewhat similar exchange took place when a client was speaking of her difficulties, yet not speaking of them directly. The counsellor was reflecting back to her what she had said the previous week, and the client became quite angry. On a few previous occasions, the client had warned the counsellor not to 'push her', and the counsellor had become somewhat careful in her reflections, so to hear this angry accusation was suddenly too much and the counsellor responded quite sharply: 'No! I'm not pushing you'. Then she heard the anger in her own statement, and she added: 'I'm sorry. I take that back. You *feel* I'm pushing you, so let's look at that'. And the client responded: 'You're right. I'm pushing myself', and went on to discuss the very topic she had been so zealously avoiding. The counsellor's congruent response enabled the client to be real in return, and focus on what she had been circling around.

In my work I will share my feelings if I believe that such expression would be helpful to my client's story, and our relationship right now. My deciders are relevance and helpfulness to the work in hand. If I reckon some disclosure would be in the best interests of the client, or if my feelings about something are so strong that they are distracting me from the client and his material, if they are causing me to lose sight of, or contact with, my client, then I will in some fashion try to share some of what I am feeling in that moment. I will choose to share rather than hide behind a mask or defence which would be incongruent. I do believe that such transparency enhances the relationship between me and my client. 'Congruence is a state of being and does not demand action.'[12]

For example, if a client is discussing a bereavement it may link into a loss of mine, recent or otherwise, and I may find it well-nigh impossible not to drift distractedly into my own pain and sadness. If I can be honest and real about this: 'I'm sorry, but when you mentioned losing your mother, I was reminded of when my own mother died. It was a tough time, and I'm aware it must be a tough time for you right now.' Any such switch is most effective if it is brief and if the focus is returned to the client almost immediately. Here I became aware of my distraction, acknowledged its force to myself, took the decision to mention it, did so, and re-focused on the client, all in a short few words. This usually succeeds in defusing my distraction, but perhaps brevity is the most important element in this self-sharing. Yalom said, 'It is counterproductive for the therapist to remain opaque and hidden from the patient',[13] but he strongly cautioned that self-disclosure must be used with discretion and with caution, in the best interests of the client. It is never a licence to merely tell your own counsellor story. Most of the time congruence is experienced by the client – and portrayed by the counsellor – as the counsellor being fully present in the relationship, in the moment of therapy: attentive and caring, accepting and real, and present.

Tolerance of uncertainty

Certainty is rare in counselling work, and being congruent means that I can acknowledge and tolerate uncertainty without feeling the need to be certain or right. If 'the aim is primarily that he should not be deceiving the client as to himself',[14] then I will be willing to admit to myself, and to my client, that I do not know, perhaps even that I too am all at sea. This does not mean, of course, that I give up and say I don't know, I cannot know, I will never know. If I can be strong enough and real enough, I can admit this uncertainty, this not knowing, and express to my client my willingness to sit with her in this dark place, while she continues to explore or allow painful feelings through. We are both striving for understanding, but even more important is my acceptance and willingness to be with her as she looks for clarity. My uncertainty can either render me ineffectual if I am embarrassed at my not knowing, or it can be a starting point for further work if I can use it to strengthen the relationship with my honesty.

'But I felt as if I had nothing to say. Indeed I could not think. My mind froze. I felt lost and muddled. My thoughts did not seem to go anywhere or connect with anything. I felt quite desperate. I was failing Johanna. I could not help. She had gone somewhere I could not reach her. With some relief, I realised that this feeling in itself was a possible place to start.'[15] 'Sitting with uncertainty' takes on new meaning at a time like this! How much easier and more comfortable to say 'Don't worry, it will come right in the end', or 'Don't be so sad, tomorrow will be better', or even 'Statistics show that most people get better over time.' Such statements come from *our* need as counsellors and human beings to be sure and certain in this uncertain world. We cannot tolerate this client's fear and pain, so we rush to reassure, to rescue, perhaps without even recognising that it is ourselves we are rescuing. The requirement here is to be congruent with ourselves, and acknowledge our own basic fears, which include a fear of being seen to be hesitant, of not knowing, of making a mistake. The ghost of the 'good' counsellor (or even the 'best' counsellor), can haunt us long after our training.

Client's perception of congruence

It is not enough to *be* congruent – the client must (to some extent at least) be aware of the counsellor as being a real, and open person. Perhaps the only way this can be achieved with a fearful, suspicious client is not to try too hard, but to be congruent and to be *consistently* congruent. Then bit by bit, session by session, over time and in response to every story, we remain our same selves. Being consistent allows for the brief flashes of impatience or dislike which all counsellors experience from time to time in response to the stories or traits of their clients – however much these may militate against our picture of a 'good' counsellor. Such flashes of annoyance need to be registered by the counsellor, for future supervision perhaps, or reference, but do not need to be spoken or highlighted in the moment. It is when these 'flashes' occur and re-occur, building up to an ongoing irritation, or a distraction from the work with the client, that they will be addressed by the counsellor in the session. The main task here is to illustrate for the client what is happening for the counsellor right here and now, never punitive or accusatory, but owned as the counsellor's material. It can then serve to illuminate and encourage exploration.

For example, when a client discloses a thought or an action that impacts strongly on us, and follows on with 'Does that shock you?', a placating response of 'Not at all. Of course not.' may carry a message of 'I am a counsellor and we are unshockable', and if we have truly been knocked back may well come across as simply not true. A response such as 'It does sound quite shocking', or 'Yes it does a bit' would ring true and real, and could be followed by '... but I cannot even begin to guess how it must have impacted on you', or 'I get the impression that it shocks you even now.'

It is obviously easy when writing or speaking outside a session to produce a satisfactory and exactly correct response, and so difficult at times within a session to convey precisely what it is we would wish to say. However, as we try for an understanding response, often our visible effort to understand and our stumbling words will carry undertones of our effort to be genuine, and to hear correctly what the client is sharing, and these will convey to our clients that we wish to be present with them to seek understanding together, even if we're not managing this very well in this moment! 'This is a reality which I find others experience as dependable.'[16] This doesn't mean sweet and loving to all clients, it means true to our present selves, not pretending and not hiding. I cannot switch this 'realness' on and off, and it will be present in all my relationships, but perhaps more concentrated in the counselling relationship, which has the client as its focus. Mearns and Thorne define congruence as 'the state of being of the counsellor when her outward responses to her client consistently match the inner feelings and sensations which she has in relation to the client.'[17]

Rogers was aware of the difficulty in being congruent when he wrote: 'It is not necessary (nor is it possible) that the therapist be a paragon who exhibits this degree of integration, of wholeness, in every aspect of his life. It is sufficient that he is accurately himself in this hour of this relationship, that in this basic sense he is what he actually is, in this moment of time ... this includes being himself even in ways which are not regarded as ideal for psychotherapy. His experience may be 'I am afraid of this client...',[18] and if the counsellor does not deny these feelings to his awareness, then he is being congruent. This paragraph was a great comfort to me when I began work as a counsellor. It seemed to encourage my attempts to be real, without being punitive, even though I fell far short of the ideal. Rogers also encapsulated the whole concept when he advocated being open and dependable and trustworthy, which 'does not demand that I be rigidly consistent but that I be dependably real.'[19]

UNCONDITIONAL POSITIVE REGARD

For Rogers, unconditional positive regard 'means a caring for the client, but not in a possessive way or in such a way as simply to satisfy the therapist's own needs. It means a caring for the client as a *separate* person, with permission to have his own feelings, his own experiences.'[20] We need to accept, unreservedly, what our client is, not what we would like her to be, not what we think she ought to be. We need to respect this different person, and *allow* her to have different values and needs and experiences from ours, and above all not to be afraid of those differences.

The basic element is to remember that my value system is *mine,* and to be careful not to impose this on my clients. How easy it is to criticise or dismiss those who have different values, or apparently none at all! I try to 'prize' the person rather than his actions or standards. For the client who has grown up with harsh conditions of worth, such acceptance can have an enormous impact. She can become emboldened to rediscover her inner self, which has been kept hidden and almost forgotten since it was perceived as unacceptable to others. Unconditional positive regard, non-judgemental positive regard, non-possessive love, acceptance – all are different words to describe our attitude of acceptance of the client 'as she is' without the expectation that she should be something other.

'Acceptance is the consistent willingness to value and respect the other as a person of worth, without conditions and without being deflected by the person's behaviour.'[21] The emphasis is on *acceptance*, and not on approval, which implies a value judgement. To approve of the behaviour or emotional state of a client would be to impose an additional condition of worth, or perceived standard of behaviour which we expect her to reach. In effect we would be saying 'I approve of you when you do such and such, and I disapprove when you do the other'. If my client believes that I am disapproving, this could reinforce her belief that she is not 'good enough', 'not up to the mark.'

My hope is that my client will gain a belief in herself and in her emotions, an acceptance of herself as she really is. I need to be sufficiently secure in myself so that I can reach out and 'hold' her in her desperation and unhappiness. I am also trying to convey my belief that she is entitled to feel thus and thus, and that I accept these feelings and will not merely try to 'kiss and make them better'. I also try to accept the struggle my clients endure to achieve change, and I try to trust and respect that struggle. Years ago someone said to me: do not try to prevent their sadness: they are entitled to their tears. At the time it sounded heartless, but I have come to agree.

Clients who are defensive, aggressive, or vulnerable people require this acceptance if they are to discover and heal the obstacles to positive self-regard which may be there since infancy. I believe that over time my client will lay aside her defences, will become real and open, and will change the protective habits of a lifetime, trusting me and herself, and becoming quite a different person in her own drama. It is a lot to ask, and self-concept change is difficult, so saying it or wishing it, or even planning it, does not automatically make it happen.

It is essential that this attitude not be merely switched on and off, and particularly that it is not 'trip-switched' by something shocking or disturbing voiced by the client. It is not an attitude that I can adopt just for client work, or work with a particular client. It needs to become a part of me, my way of being in my world, a fundamental belief that each client (each person) is unique, worthy of respect, and in whatever way, doing the best they can in this moment. This can demand a large element of trust, when a client can appear to be playing games, deliberately being obtuse, regressing, being repetitive, or whatever. It is important that I try to be consistent in my relating to, and acceptance of, my client. Blowing hot and cold, I could appear to endorse and accept some feelings but not others, and could also create new conditions of worth for a client already struggling to find freedom from the oppressive opinions she perceives others to have, or oppressive judgements she perceives others to make.

Working with a client who is angry at me, or trying to manipulate me, I find it is important to look at why this person wants to try and control me, rather than getting annoyed at the attempt. I ask myself is she afraid of me, of the work, of herself, of uncertainty?

Acceptance by me is the first step towards self-acceptance on the part of a client whose inner self-critic is particularly strong. Rogers described the process thus:

> As he finds someone listening to him with consistent acceptance ... he becomes able to listen to feelings within himself that have previously seemed so bizarre, so terrible, or so disorganising that they had been shut off completely from awareness ... He finds that the therapist's regard for him remains unshaken. And, slowly, he moves towards adopting this same attitude towards himself, towards accepting himself as he is ... towards expressing all of himself more openly. He is, at last, free to change and grow...[22]

This acceptance without judgement is essential in terms of the stated or visible attitudes and feelings of the client. But it is also essential in terms of what is not yet known, what may be revealed tomorrow. We are trying to accept the total person, known and unknown, visible and hidden, and also trying to convey this total acceptance to the client. When counsellors are in tune in this way 'they are able to convey to the client something like: "I know you feel murderous, I can even feel it within me – that does not change my sense of you as a person of worth." ... this can lead to an even deeper connection with destructive impulses ... It is when this connection is deeply felt and openly expressed that change of some kind is likely to occur'.[23] If the client is not to some extent aware of our acceptance, then fear of rejection or judgement may understandably prevent him from opening up an unpleasant aspect of himself to the counsellor's awareness, and perhaps also to his own awareness. The fear may be that such a disclosure may prove too threatening to himself, or too dangerous lest the counsellor reject or dismiss him.

The client's recorded personal message, repeated endlessly, will be: 'I will only be accepted and loved if I work hard, never get angry, do not criticise.' The basic need in us all to be loved and accepted will have copper-fastened certain rules of behaviour, of permissible emotions, so that they will have become part of 'the way I am'. (See Chapter 2.) The original critical voice will have become his own, and to risk changing that message, and therefore to risk becoming acceptable by others, will require courage, conviction, and time; 'for the time being you lay aside your own views and values in order to enter another's world without prejudice.'[24] The message of acceptance by the counsellor may be very difficult for the client to hear. But it is vital that the counsellor conveys acceptance through her efforts to be present with the client. The client may have a very poor awareness or sense of his intrinsic value as a person in his own right, and if he has built a construct about his relationships with other people, a way of relating through the belief that he is worthless and consequently holding the other person at a remove, then this will require of him a great change.

Loving or liking

'It is possible to accept the client as a person of worth while still not liking some of the things he does.'[25] Liking and disliking focus on *my* preferences for a way of being that pleases me. Liking is conditional on many factors such as whether the other person shares my values, comes from a similar background, is good fun to be with and so on. It is difficult indeed to 'like' someone who is critical of, or hostile to us. Loving incorporates wishing a person well, respecting their right to their own values and opinions, irrespective of whether they are in line with ours.

A client with a poor self-image or a negative regard for herself will not expect others to like her. Believing herself to be unloveable, and perhaps even ugly or repellant, she takes care not to reveal her true inner self to anyone else. Experience may have taught her to view people with suspicion and fear, so she reacts accordingly to others, who in turn back away from her defensiveness. Her expectations of rejection become a self-fulfilling prophecy. If the counsellor refuses to become discouraged, but stays consistently accepting while conveying the message that this client is worth listening to and worth trying to understand, perhaps the client can then begin to accept herself as well.

'The therapist perceives the client's self as the client has known it, and accepts it; he perceives the contradictory aspects which have been denied to awareness and accepts those too as being a part of the client', and as a result the client will be able to take a more tolerant attitude towards himself 'because another person has been able to adopt his frame of reference, to perceive with him, yet to perceive with acceptance and respect.'[26]

Acceptance of some clients by the counsellor can be difficult at times to achieve. For example, if I am trying constantly not to get angry with my parents, I may find it very difficult to accept those who express great rage against their mother or father. I try to perceive the inner person, often hidden and fearful, with an implacable barricade erected between himself and the world. If I succeed in sensing this inner core person, then I find myself able to wait until he can become even slightly visible. In the meantime, I remain aware of the fortress-like defences, and the salvos of avoidance, yes-buts, and sometimes even downright hostility. The hope is that my persistence and patience will create sufficient safety for the emergence of the inner person. By not behaving in the expected and accustomed manner, such as retaliating when something hurtful is said or by meeting criticism with sarcasm, I am illustrating the acceptance I am trying to convey. In some manner I am holding a space for the lost part of my client, until he finds it for himself.

This is not always successful. I once worked with a client who came regularly for six months, and spoke briskly of surface matters session after session. I could not understand why he was coming, what benefits he could be finding in our meetings, and I began to suspect that he came in order to be able to say at work: 'I was with my "analyst" at lunch time'! Today I believe I would ask him outright, and explain my own sense of the absence of his real self from the sessions, but this was in pre-supervision days. His sessions came to an end after his wife came to see me 'incognito', on the pretext of being a client herself, for just one session. (I did not make the connection with him as she used her maiden name. Quite cloak and dagger!) He came once more, and told me of her visit, and just said he felt it was time to end. I have always had a sense of being 'used' by this couple, in some intangible way, as part of some hidden game they played. (However, I must confess I also took some pleasure in believing that she looked on me as a 'threat', and in some obscure, or maybe obvious, way, this was flattering!)

Clients will often refer to different parts of themselves, the 'fun me', my 'inner child' (the 'configurations' mentioned in Chapter 2). At times we talk to these 'selves' as if we were giving instructions to someone else: 'Just walk past and pretend you don't see them', 'Come on – you can do it!', 'Count to ten', and we switch between these, adapting our various selves to whatever circumstances we find ourselves in. (These are not multiple personalities but different dimensions of the self. These configurations are known to the client, and are within her conscious awareness.) A client described his fluctuations between different aspects as 'like being on a see-saw ... one minute I hate her and could kill her, and the next I am torn up by love and pity for her. It is as if there were two separate persons on the see-saw, and one moment one was up and the next the other rose up to take charge.' The conflict and dissonance engendered by these fluctuations can be imagined, and Mearns and Thorne highlighted the tendency in us as therapists to accept only those configurations which are focused on growth and change, or the self-actualising tendency. They clearly state that 'It is important that the person-centred therapist offer an equally full therapeutic relationship to *not for growth* configurations...',[27] and they do not minimise the difficulty here for many counsellors.

If I am working with a client who is remaining within an abusive relationship, I know how hard it can be to accept that part of the client that will not choose to leave. I can slip so easily into a stance of conditional acceptance, the unspoken message being: 'I cannot accept your decision to stay. How can you?' and I can find myself even tempted to offer solutions for alternative accommodation. These 'blocking' parts which are preventing my client from moving to protect herself today, may have been crucial in protecting her earlier in life, and it is important that she explore, in safety and without criticism, *all* aspects of her self, nice and nasty, fearful and independent, positive and negative, growing and stuck.

Mearns outlines the dynamics involved in self-concept change:[28] our attitude towards our self, our self-concept, includes our beliefs, our feelings and our behaviour. It is resistant to the threat of change, because consistency and the familiar is safer than dissonance and the unknown. Exploration in counselling brings new awareness of hitherto hidden echoes of worth, and the acceptance of all aspects of the client by the counsellor. Change might require that the client regard himself as a person of value, who no longer needs to maintain the negative self-image, which has been familiar but also unhappy, for so many years. This can be frightening, requiring new responsibilities and new efforts, and it is no wonder that clients sometimes contemplate the results of change and decide to stay with the familiar. 'The great mystery of the therapeutic process is the transition between this struggle within the self-concept and actual self-concept change',[29] but we can know that it is both slow and difficult, and challenging for both client and counsellor.

A client spoke of the kindness and caring of a counsellor as being more difficult to deal with, and quite overpowering, than many other attitudes: 'At first I valued her reassurance and support a great deal. It was just what I had been wanting. After a time though, if I began to feel depressed, or ashamed, or frightened, she would rush in to rid me of these feelings. She could not seem to let me have my own feelings – to really feel them and find my own way out of them ... I guess we were trying to accomplish two different things. I was trying to grow a new personality and she was trying to patch up the old one; I was trying to let some of my real feelings out and she wanted to cover them up again.'[30]

The counsellor here was not truly listening to the client. She was following her own agenda and confusing exploration of feelings with rescuing her client from pain. Whether she herself just could not bear to listen to the hurt, or accept that this client was still ashamed or frightened, or whether she believed that she knew what was best for the client, is immaterial. The result was a frustrating struggle by the client to persuade the counsellor that it was like this right now, and that this was what she wanted to explore. It would not be surprising if in such circumstances, a client just ceased trying and went away; 'if the counsellor honestly respects the client absolutely, whatever feelings or attitudes the client has, then the client will no longer need to pretend to be other than they are, and will be released into being fully themselves, into being fully authentic.'[31]

EMPATHY

As far back as 1952 Carl Rogers was prepared to outline what he saw as essential for a good counselling relationship. His thesis was revolutionary then, and today is still a clear definition for how I am working as a counsellor: 'we do not try to do something *to* the client. We do not diagnose his case, nor evaluate his personality; we do not prescribe treatment, nor determine what changes are to be effected, nor set the goal that shall be defined as a cure. Instead the therapist ... tries to see the client as the client sees himself, to look at problems through his eyes, to perceive with him his confusions, fears and ambitions.'[32] In 1984 Rogers described the third core condition of empathy or accurate empathic understanding as 'the ability, accurately and sensitively, to understand the experiences and feelings of the client and the meanings they have for the client.'[33]

Empathy describes this effort to actively be with my client where she currently exists, to try to take part with her in her world. It does not merely involve looking *at* the client's current state of anxiety or unhappiness, no matter how efficiently we may do this. It demands a more active participation with the client's feelings and frame of reference. It is not merely the attempt to understand the recited facts which is important, but rather the attempt to grasp my client's *perception* of these facts, and the transmission to her of my effort at understanding.

And while understanding is important, it must be preceded by emotional recognition, by the grasping of what it feels like to be this person (without losing track of what it feels like to be *me*).

Where non-judgemental acceptance of a client is an attitude on my part, and congruence is my 'way of being' with the client, empathy is the active ongoing work of trying to see the client's world as if I *were* the client. Fully dependent for effectiveness on the other core conditions, it is more active in the sense that I am striving to access and occupy the other's frame of reference. We are looking *with* our client at the client's world, or as Yalom tells us 'Look out the other's window. Try to see the world as your patient sees it.'[34]

Our effort of trying to be as if in the other person's shoes is an emotional effort rather than a rational one. The rational understanding, or approximation of understanding, will follow on from the emotional recognition. It has been suggested recently that there might be 'an area in the brain that could form the basis for empathy. Not only do different neurones fire in response to different kinds of pain, but some are also triggered by seeing someone else experiencing that particular sort of pain.'[35] However, this reaction could be one of mere sympathy or pity for the other person, which may be present, but which are most certainly not the basis for empathy. My clients do not need my pity, which can suggest that 'I feel sorry for this unfortunate person.' They need acceptance of themselves as they are right now, and some belief and trust that they can change, however difficult (if not impossible) this may appear at this time.

Being with the client

Obviously I can never be fully aware of the intense inner feelings of another person, or gauge the emotional impact on another of a particular happening or event. Rogers stated that we need to try to put ourselves in the other person's shoes, as if we actually were that person. He emphasised the need also to remain aware that we can never do this fully, and never to make the mistake of believing, and saying, that we know comprehensively just how another is feeling or reacting to something. 'I know exactly how you feel' must be one of the most inaccurate, and certainly for me one of the most annoying, statements that we can make to another person. (On the other hand, the phrase has been described by Anne Simpson as being 'most comforting, a realisation that I was not the only person in the world to feel so bad and someone else shared the feeling',[36] so once again I am forced to realise that *my* reaction is mine, and is not universal!) However, we cannot know exactly how another person feels, and 'far too often we project our own feelings onto the other.'[37] We can really only know what we believe *we* would feel in a similar situation.

I find it at times difficult to remember that very often my clients are struggling to understand their own feelings, and that it is not merely in the attempt to communicate these that confusion exists. If I can be aware that the difficulty is more than just the inability to find the correct words, then I can try to facilitate clarification, identification and understanding on the client's part. (If this clarity were already available to the client, then he would probably not be in counselling at all, but would rather be managing his own life and making his own decisions.) Rogers instanced a client who said that he had spoken, or tried to speak with his friends about his difficulties but 'I was really saying the thing next to the thing that was really bothering me.'[38] As counsellor, I will try to hold the paradox of seemingly opposing feelings, love/hate, loss/relief, and try to illustrate and illuminate the possibility of tolerating it. My task is to be aware of the blockage, and to accompany my client through the fog of uncertainty and not-knowing, hopefully towards at least a lesser confusion.

'Can I sense [the client's private world] so accurately that I can catch not only the meanings of his experience which are obvious to him, but those meanings which are only implicit, which he sees only dimly or as confusion? ... even a minimal amount of empathic understanding – a bumbling and faulty attempt to catch the confused complexity of the client's meaning – is helpful.'[39] If I can perceive with respect and acceptance what my client is beginning to discover within himself, then instead of avoiding or turning away from an opaque area of threat, wherein may lie dreadful secrets or potential dangers, he may be willing to risk exploration because he is not alone in venturing towards the unknown or the hidden. Hopefully he will be able to mirror within himself my acceptance of the negative or hostile elements he is discovering within himself 'because another person has been able to adopt his frame of reference, to perceive with him, yet to perceive with acceptance and respect.'[40]

Empathy then is this willingness to enter into the private perceptual world of my clients, and to do so without being overwhelmed. 'You are a confident companion to the person in his or her inner world.'[41] At times I may have a lingering fear that, in the close connection between my own feeling knowledge and that of my client's, the danger exists of losing my own certainties and confidence, and of being somehow drawn so closely to a client that my own identity could be compromised, that I could become lost in the client's world. It is essential that I be not only aware of myself and my feeling world, but also secure in my own identity. It is imperative that I know myself as well as I can, my moods, tenses, prejudices, so that I can be aware of how *my* reactions can colour the meaning and flavour of the exchange between me and my client.

This is where supervision can be of supreme importance to me, because such confidence and security could also become a refusal or inability to be fully aware of the impact of the other, perhaps even a fear of having to face some block in my own awareness. Rogers spoke of trying to see and hear the world as our clients see and experience it. Empathy 'is extremely important both for the understanding of personality dynamics and for effecting changes in personality and behaviour. It is one of the most delicate and powerful ways we have of using ourselves.'[42]

Different levels of empathy

My ability to be empathic will obviously be different at different stages of the counselling relationship. For example, in a third session, a client who says: 'I was a bit nervous. Wouldn't anyone be?' may need a response which merely acknowledges the statement of fear. In session 20, on the other hand, when the relationship is well established, my knowledge of this client's lack of self-esteem and history of avoidance of self-searching may prompt a response such as 'I sense it's difficult for you to admit to being afraid?', or 'You've said it was an ordinary situation, and yet you've mentioned being afraid a couple of times, and I'm wondering if it reminded you of a previous time?' This latter response senses something else at the edge of the client's awareness, some unspoken feelings, which may be relevant. I am trying to acknowledge the fear, accept it without in any way judging whether the event can be abstractly labelled fearful, and facilitate exploration of the frightened reaction so that the client may come to accept the fear in himself, and then seek an understanding of it. The results of empathic interaction are of great consequence to the individual: 'empathy dissolves alienation [when] someone else knows what I am talking about.'[43] If we sense that the other person values us, then we begin to believe that we have some value. 'Empathy gives that needed confirmation that one does exist as a separate, valued person with an identity.'[44]

When I hear words, or statements, or ideas, I hold them up to the light of my experience to date. I need also to scrutinise verbal and physical clues, tone and inflection, tenseness and posture, and to infer something from these. It may be guess-work, but I can make an informed guess as to how this client is reacting emotionally to different pressures and events. However, as all our experiencing is so different, then in hearing the story of another, I may radically alter its texture and meaning when I view it through the lens of my particular experience.

Empathy is 'possibly the most potent factor in bringing about change and learning.'[45] 'Furthermore when a person is deeply understood in this way, it is difficult to maintain for long a stance of alienation and separation. Empathic understanding restores to the lonely and alienated individual a sense of belonging to the human race.'[46] In my efforts to see beneath and beyond her words, of course I need to be also constantly aware that it is easy to misread physical clues, and physical tension in my client can indicate either psychic fear or severe back pain! Like black holes in space, known by their impact on their surroundings rather than directly visible, I can sometimes infer something about a client as a result of its manifestations within her. I can of course also be wrong, but 'I have no investment in the correctness of my responses, as I attempt to understand.'[47] The simplicity of definition and of explanation can mask the supreme difficulty of *being* empathic. When I try to communicate my empathic response, I may think and hope that I am transmitting such and such an idea or emotion, but it may be received in what almost amounts to a different language. Any human verbal exchange is fraught with the potential for misunderstanding, and as the client tries to tell me of her experiences, her words can prove unreliable messengers to my understanding.

Some counsellors have a repertoire of 'empathic responses' that they use when they feel some comment is called for, in order to show solidarity with the client. Obviously it is useful outside of the sessions to consider, and practise, how we might respond in certain situations, and also to read and learn about how other counsellors make reply. However, to use such responses automatically, and to believe that we are thus being empathic, would be far off target, and could result in a caricature of empathic attitude. Without the effort and the caring intention, my words may be beautifully honed and immensely clever, but may sound to the client as merely empty and out of tune. If I am truly trying to be with my client, trying to see his world from his perspective and further trying to communicate this attempt to him, then it is likely that my inner empathic response to my client will shine through, no matter how clumsy the words I use. If an empathic response turns out to be wrong, or my client is not ready to truly hear it, I hope I will not insist: 'Oh yes you are! Oh no I'm not!' As Mearns and Thorne put it: 'Metaphorically, the person-centred counsellor wants to "knock on the client's door", but she does not want to "knock the door down"!'[48]

In trying to understand what empathy is, or in trying to *be* empathic, it is therefore important to remember that empathy is *not* the empathic response. The response is the sharing of my empathic sensing of where the client is at right now, a signpost indicating my attempt to be aware of the client's world. It is worth repeating here Roger's assertion that he is '*not* trying to "reflect feelings". I am trying to determine whether my understanding of the client's inner world is correct'.[49] Indeed, so widespread became the idea that counselling consisted merely of reflecting feelings, that the very word 'reflect' eventually became for Rogers 'a word that made me cringe.'[50] He preferred the phrases 'testing understandings' or 'checking perceptions' as he attempted to see the world from the client's perspective. In general it has been found that the responses which are most likely to be effective are those which are both flexible and appropriate to the individual client, rather than those which could be perceived on the surface as being empathic.

In effect we can only be truly empathic if we are being non-judgemental and willing to be open about ourselves, and if we care for the other person to at least some degree. Taken thus in conjunction with the other two core conditions, '…deep understanding is, I believe, the most precious gift one can give to another.'[51]

Boundaries

Boundaries provide a framework within which the work of therapy can effectively take place, and without them the relationship and the offering of the core conditions could lose much of their effectiveness. The safety of the counselling space, for both client and counsellor, depends finally on some grounding of the work, and boundaries include the nature of the relationship, time keeping and limitations, contracting or agreement of specified conditions, issues of power and so forth. Obviously these will need to be outlined to, and agreed by, the client at the start of the work. Person-centred counsellors sometimes speak of the 'fluidity' of boundaries in their way of working, and some flexibility may be required when 'responding as unique individuals *to* unique individuals.'[52] This suggests that there need not be the same strict adherence to boundary regulations as in other forms of therapy, because the central focus is on the client rather than on a structure of rules. Of course, any such departure from boundaries must be unequivocally in line with the Code of Ethics of the professional body to which the counsellor belongs, and must also be carefully thought through and justifiable. It is essential that the counsellor 'deliberate upon what is best in any given situation,'[53] and there must be no snatching at vague possibilities or experiments, but rather thoughtful flexibility in practice.

These core conditions therefore interact with each other, and underpin the special therapeutic relationship which is the core of the person-centred approach. 'Its central hypothesis is that persons have within themselves vast resources for self-understanding and for constructive changes in ways of being and behaving and that these resources can best be released and realised in a relationship with certain definable qualities.'[54] These core conditions become established, not because of what the counsellor *does*, but as a result of the counsellor's attitude towards the client. They are really only looked at separately in articles or books for discussion purposes, and the relationship is the result of all three. 'It is in their dance, their intricate interweaving, that the core conditions reveal their vitality and their potency as a healing force.'[55] 'Becoming' the three conditions enables the counsellor to be a particular type of person, who offers the opportunity to a client to enter into a particular type of relationship, which has been shown to be effective.

And I try always to remember 'my very human fallibility in understanding that client, and the occasional failures to see life as it appears to him, failures which fall like heavy objects across the intricate, delicate web of growth which is taking place.'[56] Rogers always accepted that he was not the perfect counsellor, so I can accept myself as imperfect also!

Notes

1. Howard Kirschenbaum and Valerie Land Henderson, eds., *The Carl Rogers Reader* (Constable, 1990) 16.

2. Carl Rogers and Ruth Sanford 'Client-Centered Psychotherapy' in *Comprehensive Textbook of Psychiatry*, IV Eds. H.I. Kaplan and B.J. Sadock (Williams and Wilkins Co., Baltimore, 1984) 1378.

3. David Cohen *Carl Rogers – A Critical Biography* (Constable, 1997) 13.

4. Celia Homan *Eisteach: A Quarterly Journal of Counselling and Psychotherapy* published by Irish Association for Counselling and Psychotherapy Vol. 2, No. 24 Spring 2003 24.

5. Dave Mearns and Brian Thorne *Person-Centred Counselling in Action* (Sage, 1999) 22.

6. Brian Thorne *Carl Rogers* (Sage, 1992) 46.

7. Carl R. Rogers *On Becoming a Person* (Constable, 1961) 12.

8. Carl R. Rogers 'Some learnings from a study of psychotherapy with schizophrenics' in C.R. Rogers and B. Stevens *Person to Person* (Lafayette, CA Real People Press) 181-191.

9. Dave Mearns and Brian Thorne *Person-Centred Counselling in Action* (Sage, 1999) 85.

10. Carl R. Rogers 'The Case of Mrs Oak' in *Psychotherapy and Personality Change* Eds., C.R. Rogers and R.F. Dymond (University of Chicago Press, Chicago, 1954) 33.

11. Dave Mearns and Brian Thorne *Person-Centred Counselling in Action* (Sage, 1999) 91-2.

12. Paul Wilkins *Person-Centred Therapy in Focus* (Sage, 2003) 82.

13. Irvin D. Yalom *The Gift of Therapy* (Piatkus, 2002) 83.

14. *The Carl Rogers Reader* Eds. Howard Kirschenbaum and Valerie Land Henderson (Constable, 1990) 224.

15. Susie Orbach *The Impossibility of Sex* (Penguin, 1999) 69.

16. Carl R. Rogers *On Becoming a Person* (Constable, 1961) 50.

17. Mearns and Thorne *Person-Centred Counselling in Action* (Sage, 1999) 84

18. *The Carl Rogers Reader* Eds. Howard Kirschenbaum and Valerie Land Henderson (Constable, London, 1990) 224.

19. Ibid., 11.

20. Ibid., 225.

21. Dave Mearns and Brian Thorne *Person-Centred Therapy Today* (Sage,

2000) 201.

22. Carl R. Rogers and Ruth C. Sanford *'Client-Centered Psychotherapy'* 1381.

23. Paul Wilkins *Person-Centred Therapy in Focus* (Sage, 2003) 63.

24. Carl R. Rogers *A Way of Being* (Houghton Mifflin Co. Boston, 1980) 143.

25. Mearns and Thorne *Person-Centred Counselling in Action* 65.

26. Carl R. Rogers *Client-Centered Therapy* (Constable, 1951) 41.

27. Mearns and Thorne *Person-Centred Therapy Today* 115.

28. Dave Mearns *Developing Person-Centred Counselling* (Sage, 1994) 88-93.

29. Ibid., 91.

30. William H. Fitts *The Experience of Psychotherapy: What It Is Like for Client and Therapist* Van Nostrand Reinhold (Princeton NJ, 1965) 29.

31. *Person-Centred Therapy – A European Perspective* Eds. Brian Thorne and Elke Lambers Sage UK 1998 25.

32. Reprinted from *The Scientific American*, 448 Nov. 52 W.H.Freeman and Co. USA 3 and 4.

33. Carl R. Rogers and Ruth C. Sanford *'Client-Centered Psychotherapy'*: Article in *Comprehensive Textbook of Psychiatry*, IV Eds. H.I. Kaplan and B.J. Sadock (Williams and Wilkins Co., Baltimore, 1984) 1378.

34. Irvin D. Yalom *The Gift of Therapy* (Piatkus, 2002) 18.

35. Financial Times, 3 June 2000 Jerome Burne 'Tip to Toe'.

36. Anne Simpson: Personal statement to author.

37. Irvin D. Yalom *The Gift of Therapy* Piatkus Pubs., USA 2002 21.

38. Carl. R. Rogers *Client-Centered Therapy* (Constable, London 1951) 51.

39. *The Carl Rogers Reader* Eds. Howard Kirschenbaum and Valerie Land, Henderson (Constable, London 1990) 121-122.

40. Carl R. Rogers *Client-Centered Therapy* (Constable, London 1951) p 41.

41. Carl R. Rogers *A Way of Being* (Houghton Mifflin Co. Boston, 1980) 142.

42. Ibid., 137.

43. Ibid., 151.

44. Ibid., 155.

45. Ibid., 139.

46. Dave Mearns and Brian Thorne *Person-Centred Counselling in Action*

(Sage, 1999) 15.

47. *The Carl Rogers Reader* Eds. Howard Kirschenbaum and Valerie Land Henderson (Constable, London 1990) 141.

48. Dave Mearns and Brian Thorne *Person-Centred Counselling in Action* (Sage, 1999) 47.

49. *The Carl Rogers Reader* Eds. Howard Kirschenbaum and Valerie Land Henderson, (Constable, London, 1990) 27.

50. Carl R. Rogers *A Way of Being* (Houghton Mifflin Boston, 1980) p 138.

51. Ibid., 161

52. Paul Wilkins *Person-Centred Therapy* in Focus (Sage, 2003) 130.

53. Ibid., 131.

54. Carl R. Rogers and Ruth C. Sanford '*Client-Centered Psychotherapy*': in *Comprehensive Textbook of Psychiatry*, IV Eds. H.I. Kaplan and B.J. Sadock (Williams and Wilkins Co., Baltimore 1984) 1374.

55. Dave Mearns and Brian Thorne *Person-Centred Therapy Today* (Sage, 2000) 86.

56. *The Carl Rogers Reader* Eds. Howard Kirschenbaum and Valerie Land Henderson (Constable, London, 1990) 6.

7

Elizabeth

'It is axiomatic that whatever one anticipates in therapy is never quite what happens.'[1]

Elizabeth
When I consider my client Elizabeth, my memory is one of haste and hurry, which is strange because our sessions at the time appeared if anything leisurely and thoughtful. I have since wondered if she came to counselling at a time when she was very ready for it, if she had her thinking already done about where she would like to go, and if she used counselling to clarify her ideas into words, and thence into actions. There was a sure-footedness about her work, in hindsight, that make me wonder if unconsciously she had already previewed change and found it acceptable.

Session 1
Elizabeth was a forty-seven-year-old married woman who made and cancelled two appointments before finally coming to session 1. When I greeted her, she quickly said, 'Call me Betty. Everyone else does', and there was something in the way she said it that suggested that she didn't like it, but people did it

anyway, as if her wishes didn't matter. It seemed important to ask, 'What would you *like* me to call you?' and she said that she actually liked the name Elizabeth. It was a small thing, but it felt like a good start.

Elizabeth launched immediately into her story, and why she had come. Married for almost nine years, she had no children, and I was startled when she added emphatically, 'Thank God!' She lived about twenty miles outside Dublin and her husband, Paul, commuted to the city every day. Some months before she had been told by a friend that Paul had been seeing someone else in Dublin, under the disguise of long, hard-working hours, for almost all of their married life. When she queried this with him, he admitted it as if it were something of little consequence.

I do not have a great recollection of me as a counsellor in these sessions, and I remember little of what I said. In fact I do not think I said much, yet I do have a remembered sense of being a participant rather than an onlooker.

Elizabeth: He just said 'yes, it's true,' as if I'd asked him was the news on at nine o'clock. He admitted so casually to treachery, dishonesty; he trashed our relationship and our nine years together just like that! I remember just looking at him, as if I had never seen him before, and my first thought was 'She's welcome to him.' Then it really hit me and I threw the head, shouted and yelled at him, and he just walked out and didn't come back until the next evening.

What she said was very controlled and very bleak, and each sentence was given reluctantly, small piece by small piece, as if she were giving away pieces of her soul – and maybe she was.

Her GP had suggested counselling, as she was not sleeping and was on a mild anti-depressant.

Elizabeth: He called it reactive depression, and I know I have low self-esteem. I've read a few books about psychotherapy, and wondered about doing a course in cognitive-behavioural therapy? What do you think?

Me: I'm aware that you've thought quite a lot about coming for counselling, and I'm hoping it will bring you what you're looking for.

Elizabeth: I'm looking for answers, and I don't suppose you're going to give them to me. Perhaps I can find a few of my own.

Elizabeth had appeared compliant and without much personal power at the start, but as the session went on, I became aware that it was very important for her to let me know that she knew quite a lot about counselling, that she would not be patronised or treated as a 'patient', and that above all she was not going to tolerate being pitied. Clients who present for counselling may be looking for help for the first time in their life, and may even feel it is 'degrading' or 'like begging', as two clients admitted. At the beginning of the relationship, they may even attempt to browbeat or intimidate the counsellor, in an effort to show her that they are people of consequence, at least her equal, and that they too know a thing or two about theory! This show of 'strength' does not usually continue, when the counsellor demonstrates that they are accepting of this person and not playing at being expert, just intent on listening to the client's story.

During the next three sessions she told me about her life before the break-up, which appeared to constitute a watershed in her life and her story. She had two sisters and one brother, her parents were dead and she worked in a local supermarket. There was something she needed to tell me, but she found it very difficult, could not find the words, perhaps next session. She was so ashamed and had never told anyone, not even Paul. It can be difficult to hold the waiting space until it is safe enough for the client to make the great effort to break the silence of years, and it is also difficult not to imagine that some awful scenario will be shared.

Elizabeth told her story well, with a quirky turn of phrase. It was interesting and entertaining, and I had to remain aware that it also contained the seeds of a great sadness, a mystery, and the human predicament that brought her to seek help.

Session 4
Elizabeth spoke of her childhood without much expression.

Elizabeth: It was a small village, and it was very important that no *scéal* (story) be told outside the house. I remember my mam and dad always rowed in whispers, which seemed more vicious than out and out shouting matches, which my friend's parents had. My dad spoke a lot about being in 'good standing' in the neighbourhood, which I never really understood when I was small. I had some notion about standing up tall, and I wasn't very big for my age, so somehow I was lacking. And mam was very religious, and spoke a lot about offending God. Everything we did seemed to offend God – loud music, running down the street, making fun of the parish priest. That was a really bad sin, but he did look funny, very skinny, with a very deep voice. I remember it was better outside the house than in, but there wasn't much fun anywhere. (This was said with great sadness.)

Me: It sounds tough for a small child.

Elizabeth: It sure was. I used to be afraid of going round a corner because I thought God might appear and tell me I was bad. I think I was a sneaky child, creeping around and whispering, and watching – always watching. In school I kept my head down, and managed to keep up with the others, but only just.

Me: I get the sense that you were trying to be pretty well invisible.

I was trying hard to see the world as it had appeared to the small child that had been Elizabeth, and still was in the recesses of her being.

Elizabeth: That just describes it. I used to fantasise about having a cloak that made you invisible and then I was disappointed when people spoke to me, when they could see I was really there. And yet bad and all as it was at times, it only got worse when I went into secondary school. One of the girls told me the facts of life when I was thirteen, and I thought this couldn't be true so I screwed up my courage, and asked my mam. God, she blew up – told me I was dirty, filled with bad thoughts, must go to confession and on and on.

Me: So you learned early on that sex was 'dirty'?

Elizabeth: (bitterly) She didn't even mention the word sex. That
            would have been too much altogether!

Elizabeth told me about her mother's many miscarriages,
which were never really explained, about the sudden death of
her maternal grandparents in a car accident when she was five
and of her mother appearing to withdraw from the family for
months afterwards.

Elizabeth: Mam used to speak about lost babies, and then how
            she had lost her mam and dad, and for years I
            thought they were only 'lost', and that if I looked
            hard enough, perhaps I could find them, and then
            they'd think I was great. Children really are daft, the
            things they think. As the eldest I used to think it was
            my job to make sure the younger three weren't also
            'lost'. I think I used to worry a lot.

Me: Sounds like a lot of responsibility for a small child to
            take on.

Elizabeth: And then as they grew up, the others went their own
            ways, home and abroad. I was left responsible for the
            parents when they got sick. Mam and Dad died with-
            in six months of each other eight years ago, just after
            I was married. We lived quite close, but it was a lot
            of nursing for almost a year. It didn't make for a
            good beginning to married life, but the idea of a
            nursing home wouldn't have been tolerated in the
            village, and anyway Paul was dead against it. I've

wondered was he carrying on even then, and maybe it suited him to have me occupied.

I made few interventions in this session because Elizabeth appeared to want to just tell me her story.

Sessions 5 and 6

During these two sessions, Elizabeth continued to look back at her childhood, and the sense of sadness grew, until it seemed to me out of all proportion to what she was telling me. She wept a little, and the weight of misery was almost tangible. I would not have been surprised if she had not come again, as her struggle between wanting or needing to tell how it was for her, and her inability to find words was very powerful. If I was feeling this as painful, what must it be like for Elizabeth?

Session 6

Elizabeth: (After a long silence) There is something else I'd like to tell you, but I just cannot. I feel gagged – it's horrible – I've never said it. (And she struggled and failed to find the words.)

Me: Is this something you would like me to know? (I 'borrowed' this phrase from one of my students, as an attempt to slightly shift focus from something she felt she *had* to do, to something she would like to do for someone else.)

Elizabeth: Yes, but you're just sitting there looking at me!

Me: I can feel how hard it is for you. Would it be easier if you turned your chair away, or if I sat beside you? (I

felt I had become 'the public', and that the eye contact that was so valuable most of the time had
become a searchlight. She did turn away so that she
was speaking directly into the fire.)

Elizabeth: (In a very low and rapid voice) When I was sixteen,
my friend's cousin visited from Dublin. We all
thought he was great, and he took a fancy to me. We
used to take walks on our own, and – you know – it
went too far. It was very secret and I was so caught
up with him. And of course after a few weeks he
went home and I was devastated. Then I was getting
sick, and Mam brought me to the doctor, who told
her I was pregnant. He never told me, he said nothing to me, as if I didn't exist. He told Mam while I
just listened. And at first I was delighted, just for a
couple of days. Scared, yes, but I was going to have
someone of my own, and I was making plans about
how I'd manage school, and what I'd buy for her – I
just knew it would be a girl. And the rage and the
rows didn't seem to matter. Mam told Dad and I was
sworn to secrecy. Within two weeks I was in
England and had had an abortion. Mam came with
me, and I swear she didn't speak for the whole time
we were there, just said if I ever told anyone the family would be ruined, and I'd have that on my con-
science as well as my awful sin. She made me go to
confession in England so that I wouldn't have to tell
the priest at home.

There was a long, long pause, during which I was tempted to
say how sorry I was for the young girl she had been, to say

she'd feel better now that she had told me, to say anything at all to show how well I was listening and was willing to be there with her. But of course there was really nothing to be said.

Elizabeth: She'd be thirty years old now, and maybe she'd have her own children. I never even gave her a name. (And Elizabeth looked bleakly back at the loss of both child and grandchildren, and I thought my heart would break.) And it was never spoken of again. I tried a couple of times to say something to my mother, but she wouldn't have it. I remember the last time I tried she said 'I won't talk about it. It's dead and gone' and it felt so cruel. Dead and gone. And Dad, well I could never talk to him anyway. He just got angry and started to shout, about anything I thought was important, whether it was about me or the family, or local politics even. Only the weather was safe.

I really felt we had met in this session. I felt it was very early in our relationship for such a revelation, but obviously Elizabeth came ready to trust me, and ready to face her deep unhappiness. I try to keep myself present for the client, at a meeting place in our relationship with an invitation to the client to join me there. At times clients decline to do so, or are unable to do so, and there is no real connection between us. If I were to give up and cease to be present in that place, then the client would never find it. If I manage to stay there, then in time or after an emotional breakthrough, we can meet, and in that intangible moment, the client can see possibilities of change or growth, or perhaps even her own potential self.

It was very hard to end this session, but Elizabeth looked relieved when I said that our time was up. It is so tempting to prolong a session when it has been so sad, but the client needs to know that the previously agreed length of time still holds, and it can also provide an 'escape' from the intensity of a session. She appeared to leave with a lighter step, but perhaps this was merely me consoling myself!

Session 7
In session 7, Elizabeth was determined not to refer back to her shared secret of the previous week, as if the exposure had been too great to linger with, or she wasn't yet sure of my reaction. She spoke almost casually about her partner's affair, and I felt she was checking me out, to see if my regard for and acceptance of her had changed in light of her 'revelation'. When she found me unchanged, she was able to refer to it again in session 8.

Session 8
Elizabeth started talking as she came in.

Elizabeth: I really don't know why I've told you about all this old stuff. I really came in the first place to think of what I wanted to do about Paul and his woman.

I wasn't sure if Elizabeth was looking for reassurance that it was alright to talk about 'old stuff' or if she was hoping to avoid looking back again. I wondered whether or not to move with her away from the pain she had expressed with such difficulty. The phrase 'The past casts a long shadow' echoed in my head and it seemed to fit here, so I went with my instinct.

Me: I'm hearing of so many losses – loss of safety when you were small, of babies and grandparents, of your own baby and of your parents, and now apparently the loss of Paul. To me it sounds like it's the last straw.

And as if a dam had broken she wept and wept.

Elizabeth: (After a long silence) I've been looking back at my life. And I seem to have been avoiding grief for ever. I was afraid that if I started crying, I'd never stop. So many tears inside.

And for the rest of the session she cried bitterly, and I just sat with her.

Sessions 9-11

In session 9, Elizabeth had shifted again, and spoke at length about her life with Paul, and how it had not 'been great in the bedroom department'.

Me: The bedroom department?

Elizabeth: You know, in bed. Sex. He wasn't much interested, and part of me would be relieved, and part felt I was missing something. Mostly I think I just wanted to be held and cuddled and if I had to have sex to get that, well and good. But when we did make love, he'd just 'perform' and go off to sleep. I never guessed why. I really was stupid.

Me: It sounds kind of functional.

Elizabeth: It was – and lonely too. Like he was only half there
and I'd no-one I could talk to.

She had been blaming herself for not being a 'good' wife in the
accepted sense, and she was beginning to see that it takes two to
make a good relationship. She reviewed all his faults over the last
years, and in some way the focus was shifting from herself to
Paul.

Session 12

Elizabeth: (Elizabeth was strong and confident in this session)
I'm not going to let him off the hook. I don't really
care if he goes on seeing her, but I'm not leaving the
house. He can live there and pay the bills. I'll cook
and wash, but that's all. I'll live my own life as I
please. It will be like being single, but my way will be
paid. And if he doesn't like that, then I'll tell everyone
in the town, and see how that suits him!

She continued discussing future plans, which contained a large
element of revenge and threatened disclosure, which did not sit
easily with me. I empathised with her sadness and her feelings of
betrayal, and was glad that she was allowing expression of her
anger, but I hoped she would not become merely punitive and bitter. This would not have been the outcome I would have wished
for her, but I needed to accept her in her planning and fighting for
independence. Whether I liked these or not was immaterial; it
was important that I stay with her as she struggled to cope with
the new direction her life was taking. Making what she could of
what she had left, having lost so much, would require all her new-
found strength and focus on herself. But it was something of a
struggle for me not to become judgemental of her in these plans,

and Elizabeth certainly did not need to lose me or my respect and acceptance in addition to all her other losses.

Session 15

Elizabeth: (Elizabeth came on time and began briskly) I want this to be our last session, because I feel I've gained so much that I can manage on my own now.

I was quite taken aback, as I had had no inkling that this was coming.

Elizabeth: I'm sleeping better and my doctor has reduced the pills. I've a clearer picture of where I am, and I no longer think I'm going mad. You may think this is crazy though – I've signed up at the local community college for art classes! Imagine, art classes, me! I've been to two already and we have great fun, and all the others are very nice. And the teacher is great, not a bit like being at school. Though I did win a prize for art when I was twelve. (There was a pause and I honestly could not think what to say.) You don't say much, do you? What do you really think of all this – of me and what I'm planning to do?

Elizabeth had surprised me and now her challenge to give an opinion of her and her new departures called for a truly congruent response. I wanted to trust her and her decisions, her ability to organise her life, even if I did not much like her plans or her reasons for them.

Me: To be honest, it does seem a lot of change in a short time. I'm aware you're angry with Paul and with life in general, but I'm a bit afraid for you in the speed of your decisions and what you're planning to do.

Elizabeth: (After a long silence) I'm glad you're afraid for me. I don't know when anyone has said that in years. It makes me feel kind of looked out for – that I'm not all alone. I also hear you saying that you're not going to try and change my mind, and that's both frightening and challenging at the same time. I don't feel too alone but I do feel responsible – for me anyway. I'm just not going to lie down any more – my turn now.

For Elizabeth, her losses had been 'dealt with', and her anger and her feeling that she had wasted so much of her life to date were now fuelling her actions. She was determined to end, there and then, so I told her that if she ever wanted to reconnect, or if life became difficult again, she was free to contact me. We spoke for the rest of the session about her plans in unemotional phrases, and I was tempted to say 'Please don't go. You're not ready', but of course I did not. The words 'flight into health' rang in my ears, but she was her own person, making her own decisions, and I respected that.

Elizabeth did come back a year later, and worked for approximately another eighty sessions, exploring and consolidating her progress. When she left again, she had moved from being controlled and compliant to what Rogers would surely have termed a person on the way to becoming 'fully functioning'. She had succeeded impressively in becoming a person who made choices for herself, and who had learned to accommodate a balance between her ability to look after others and her own fulfillment. She was actively pursuing a new career, she had met a new partner, and she was no longer bitter. She appeared to be happier in her 'new' life, and I certainly was happier when she left the second time.

Notes

1. Susie Orbach *The Impossibility of Sex* (Penguin, 1999) 68.

8

Spirituality

'...the voice of the mind and feelings might be so loud that the whisperings of soul and spirit are unheard.'[1]

Fourth condition

The person-centred approach bases its effectiveness on the counselling relationship characterised by the three core conditions, congruence, unconditional acceptance and empathy, but in his later years Rogers wrote briefly about a further element in this work which he admitted he had neglected up to this – a spiritual element. He indicated that this additional characteristic might be of equal importance to the other three:

> When I am at my best ... I discover another characteristic. I find that when I am closest to my inner, intuitive self, when I am somehow in touch with the unknown in me, when perhaps I am in a slightly altered state of consciousness in the relationship, then whatever I do seems to be full of healing. Then simply my *presence* is realising and helpful. There is nothing I can do to force this experience, but when I can relax and be close to the transcendental core of me, then I may behave in strange and

impulsive ways in the relationship, ways which I cannot justify rationally, which have nothing to do with my thought processes. But these strange behaviours turn out to be *right*, in some odd way. At these moments it seems that my inner spirit has reached out and touched the inner spirit of the other. Our relationship transcends itself, and has become a part of something larger. Profound growth and healing and energy are present ... I realise that this account partakes of the mystical. Our experiences, it is clear, involve the transcendent, the indescribable, the spiritual. I am compelled to believe that I, like many others, have underestimated the importance of this mystical, spiritual dimension.[2]

This insight, at the very end of his life, has not been wholeheartedly welcomed by all person-centred counsellors, but Rogers called this spiritual realm the 'next great frontier of learning', which he saw as the gateway to 'the area of the intuitive, the psychic, the vast inner space that looms before us.'[3] Thorne, too, suggests that the counselling relationship is where neglected spiritual yearnings can be nourished and sustained. 'The evidence, I believe, is overwhelming that Rogers in his deep respect for human beings and in his trust of the actualising tendency has enabled many to discover that at the deepest centre of the person and infusing the organismic self is the human spirit which is open to the transcendent.'[4]

The whole person
The PCA attempts to deal with the whole person of the client, while simultaneously trying to employ every facet of the counsellor: what do I *think* of this client and her dilemmas; what *feelings* within me respond to her sadness, her anger; do I find it

hard to *sit still* as I see her restlessness; am I in any way *sexually* attracted to her; do I find myself with an *image* that I know is not coming from within me; do I have an *intuitive* guess about her difficulties? All add up to a most complicated relationship! I do not believe, as some counsellors do, that counselling is primarily a spiritual endeavour, but neither do I agree with those who claim that spirituality has no place within the counselling room. Can I sit with one client who explores her deep relationship with God, with another who has no religious beliefs whatsoever, with a third who concentrates on the impact of Celtic spirituality on her life? Of overall importance for me is that I do not, in any way, try to impose my beliefs on my client, but that I remain always open to and conscious of what may lie beyond that which is visible or audible, beyond what she thinks, or does or says. If clients do not directly mention or discuss this aspect of their 'persona', it is essential that I remain always open to this possibility (as indeed to so many other possibilities!)

John McLeod suggests that the narrative nature of counselling, and the 'talking therapies' in general, 'omit any reference to spiritual experience, and thus deny what is for many people a primary source of meaning and belonging.'[5] It is important that I be aware of my own spiritual values, lest they unwittingly intrude on those of my clients. 'We need to be clear about our own feelings about spirituality and God... Psychotherapy and spirituality can meet very well in some ways'.[6] The counsellor who wishes to be fully present in the relationship is aware that this demands his whole self including the ethical and spiritual elements of his being. 'To embrace all these feelings and values within a unified response to another person is demanding enough, but to give expression to them without lapsing into moralism on the one hand or empty permissiveness on the other is perhaps the stiffest challenge that

any counsellor can face.'[7] Looking at my own work, I sometimes ask myself am I overly cautious in referring to spiritual
matters or people's beliefs, fearful lest I seem to be imposing
'religious' beliefs on my clients? Am I not declining to accept
the universality of the spiritual element within us all, because
of my knowledge that not everyone has a religious interest? If
it is 'unfashionable' to speak about religion in many settings,
am I too careful as to how I express my own beliefs even when
asked directly by a client? These are questions which I ask
myself, and while the answers will be as individual as the counsellors, the questions are universal.

Years ago, one of my clients who was a teacher spoke for
many sessions about her work, her childhood and how she saw
her future in teaching, but somehow we did not discuss her
present state. I had a picture of her when she was small, and of
how she might be as she grew older, but she herself remained
intangible in the sessions. I managed to accept her in this half
visibility, and wait for her to come fully into our sessions. One
day, after perhaps ten sessions, she told me she was a member
of a religious order, and went on to say that she had not been
sure if I would work with her as an individual or as a religious
sister. She wanted to be seen as a person in her own right and
was afraid that I would either be put off or focus too exclusively on her religion, (and for all I know, she may have been right!)
I do try not to allow my own explorations to intrude, but at
times clients can link into (and disturb) my own lack of knowledge, and send me searching again along different avenues. I am
content with this because, for myself, I would prefer to go to a
counsellor who has doubts, and is still asking questions, rather
than work with someone who is very sure of all the answers!

Unfortunately, if I hesitate to follow my client's lead into the
spiritual content of her work and her exploration, I may also be

negating part of my own experience of the spiritual element of me as a counsellor. This could result in a double loss of connection, a whole area ignored or not heard because of my fear of being clumsy or embarrassing. My client may have heard my hesitation as conveying the message that religion or spirituality is not an area open for discussion, and refrained from including an important part of her. Instead of observing other people through the spectacles of theory and abstraction, 'What was needed was … a spontaneous sympathy of our unconscious with that of others, a feeling response of our soul to theirs.'[8]

Generally people are hungry for, or at least aware of, truth, goodness, beauty, love – elements outside our physical material selves, and originating in 'a spiritual centre of identity.'[9] Most of us seek more than humdrum materialism and the very words 'retail therapy' are a contradiction in terms. The French philosopher Blaise Pascal pinpointed something of the spiritual when he wrote: 'The heart has its reasons, of which reason knows nothing.' In discussing unconditional regard, or respect for others, Campbell Punton suggests that in doing so we relate to their spiritual nature, to the 'something more' which lies beyond their actions. 'By a spiritual nature I mean what I think has traditionally been meant by this, namely, that the nature of persons cannot be wholly elucidated in terms of their lives 'in this world', that there is a dimension to personal existence that goes 'beyond this life'.[10]

Inner world

For me, 'spiritual' refers to what we value outside ourselves, the intangible, that feeling of awareness of we know not what. We often lack trust in our inner knowing, in our intuition, that instinctive knowledge or belief obtained neither by perception nor reason. Generally we have not been encouraged to listen to, and articulate, the spiritual, the unseen, the 'hunch' that we too often do not consider. Our inner lives can be in direct opposition to factual acceptance and recounting of our practical story, and what we sense inwardly can be too readily dismissed, even by ourselves. 'Something was telling me to get out of there', 'I had an uneasy feeling, but it wasn't based on anything concrete'. We lack a vocabulary for describing this inner world, this 'heartfelt sense', and very often cannot find the words which ring true. In our training of counsellors, spirituality is rarely given its rightful place as a vital and very real element of the person of the trainee, or her potential clients.

'Spirituality refers to the understanding of the fundamental meaning of existence and the experiences which relate to that essence of life – the absolute.'[11] Much of counselling is practical, dealing with the here and now, listening to the echoes of the past, the voices within ourselves and within our clients. We need at the same time to allow for hope and mystery by being open to the spiritual part of the client. Rogers further elaborates on the point at which this dimension was apparent with clients: 'This sensitive empathy is so deep that my intuition takes over at one point and, in a way which seems mysterious, is in touch with a very important part of her with which she has lost contact.'[12] The counsellor at such times is working in an atmosphere of imagination and possibility. Rogers was clear that 'There is nothing I can do to force this experience', but he believed that the more congruent the counsellor can be, the more likely it is that such moments will come about, touching on the mystery of our own selves and our interconnectedness with each other.

The person-centred way of working, with its concentration on uncovering the client's potential rather than offering solutions from outside, is echoed in this quotation: 'a person's journey, particularly into spiritual growth and the search for meaning, can only be addressed and realised in the individual's own natural evolution.'[13] Spirituality is a uniquely personal experience and religion is a belief system to which I may subscribe, or which I may adopt, in my search for the spiritual. I once worked with a young man who was reared in the Catholic Church and had come to a point where he had left, but had taken with him the values he had learned. He came for counselling because he had an acute sense of loss of certainty, and found life difficult because he had no one to tell him what was right or wrong, what was the best decision to make, and he was filled with guilt if he 'stepped out of line' as he saw it. He felt he had lost contact with God, because he no longer attended church services, and he felt cut off and adrift. It took a long time for him to reach a place where he could set his own standards and make his own decisions, and trust himself to live freely. Eventually he was able to adopt his own value system, and he was amazed at its similarity to the values he had grown up with, the difference being that he did not feel they were 'imposed' on him, and therefore to be resented. He succeeded in making some contact with his inner spiritual self, which he had not really considered up to now. By the time he left, after many long and tortured sessions, he was happier and more able to be 'whole' in his life, his work and his relationships.

Obviously some clients have no religious background whatsoever, but are either deeply spiritual or consumed by a longing to explore what they have labelled as their 'spiritual self'. Offering the core conditions and a place of safety allows them to stumble through their uncertainties with varying degrees of 'success'. Other people come for counselling, and express neither knowledge of nor interest in anything other than those aspects of their selves where they feel pain or disorganisation.

It is for me, as well as for my clients, uncharted territory, but to truly hear these 'whisperings of the soul and spirit' requires creative imagination and the recognition and acknowledgement of images. Assagaoli's psychosynthesis looks on 'the person from the perspective of well being and spiritual experiences.'[14] Exploration of the spiritual nature of our clients could possibly lead to it being used as a defence and a source of alienation from reality, and the avoidance of responsibility. Alienation from any part of ourselves creates dissonance and anxiety. Empowerment of the individual can run contrary to what some clients look on as their spiritual or religious beliefs, and they may merely submit to what life brings: 'lapsing into a "this is God-given" passivity, rather than dealing with matters in our lives.'[15] In our enthusiasm it is important to remember that, just as we cannot ignore the spiritual in our work, neither can we focus on it exclusively. To exclude the ordinary and the mundane would be sterile in its own way.

In partial illustration of this, I recall another client, who told me in his first sentence that he was a priest, and from there on presented me with a priestly image of himself. He told me of his work, castigated himself for what he saw as lapses in caring for parishioners, and preached at me for many sessions. I waited, but finally pointed out that I had no picture of his inner self, and that I sensed that he found it difficult to allow his own feelings and opinions to surface. He was very taken aback, but rallied to tell me that his 'self' was not important in his eyes, and that he really thought he was dealing with his difficulties. He tried very hard to understand what I meant during a few more meetings, but then the course he was doing ended, and so did his counselling. I have always felt that I somehow failed him, as I did not suggest that he was working at his religion, rather than exploring his self, or his own spiritual nature. Perhaps if I had articulated my sense of this difference, it would have helped him to contact his buried inner self.

As a counsellor, I try to remember that the spiritual is a component of the totality of my client, whether it is overtly referred to by the client, or not. 'I now consider it possible that each of us is a continuing spiritual essence lasting over time.'[16] However, it is imperative that I do not try to guide my client to consider her spirituality, in the same way as I will never 'guide' her to consider other aspects of herself that she is not ready to consider.

'It is impossible for the roles of psychiatry, psychology and counselling to ignore for much longer that we are in essence spiritual beings having human experiences.'[17] Thorne also looks at the future of the client-centred approach and believes that it will not depend on new theories of skills or techniques, but rather on '...the ability of client-centred therapists to be congruent in ways which give access to the fullness of being where language is inadequate and where we must make do with such words as mystical, spiritual and transcendent'.[18] There is a real challenge in this statement, which may well be the basis of much future work, not only in the person-centred counselling tradition, but also in the field of counselling in Ireland.

Notes

1. M. O'Regan in *Psychotherapy in Ireland*, ed., Edward Boyne (Columba Press, 2003) 81.
2. Howard Kirschenbaum and Valerie Land Henderson, eds., *The Carl Rogers Reader* (Constable, 1990) 137.
3. Stephen Palmer and Ved Varma, eds., *The Future of Counselling and Psychotherapy* (Sage, 1997) 160.
4. Brian Thorne *Carl Rogers* (Sage, 1992) 105.
5. Pat Milner and Stephen Palmer, eds., *The BACP Counselling Reader Vol. 2* (Sage, in association with BACP, 2001) 595.
6. Caoimhe O'Flynn in *Eisteach Vol. 2, 8* (Spring, 1999) 4-5.

7. Brian Thorne *Person-Centred Counselling* (Whurr Publications, 1991) 124.
8. Bruno Bettelheim *Freud and Man's Soul* (Flamingo, 1985) 5.
9. Milner and Palmer, eds., *The BACP Counselling Reader Vol. 2* 90.
10. Brian Thorne and Elke Lambers, eds., *Person-Centred Therapy – A European Perspective* (Sage, 1998) 32.
11. Ger Murphy in *Eisteach, Vol. 2,8* (Spring 1999) 20.
12. Kirschenbaum and Land Henderson *The Carl Rogers Reader* 150.
13. Pat Milner & Stephen Palmer, Eds. the BACP Counselling Reader, Vol: 2 (in assoc with BACAP, 2001) 182.
14. Boyne *Psychotherapy in Ireland* 76.
15. Susan Lindsay talking to Frances McDonnell in *Eisteach Vol. 2,8* 30.
16. Carl Rogers in Kirschenbaum and Land Henderson *The Carl Rogers Reader* 53.
17. Michael Corry 'Soul Healing' in *Eisteach Vol. 2,11* 12.
18. Brian Thorne *Person-Centred Counselling* 187.

9

Trust

'The greater the extent that therapists honor the authority of clients as the authority of their own lives then the greater the probability of constructive personality change and problem resolution.'[1]

Elements of trust

'The person-centred approach is built upon a basic trust in the person. This is perhaps its sharpest point of difference from most of the institutions in our culture.'[2]

This special trust has five components. The most obvious element is that the client needs to trust in the counsellor, or she will not be willing to explore and share at a deep level. The PCA counsellor will also trust her client and her potential, her innate ability to know what 'hurts', and to uncover the steps needed for healing. The three further elements are that the counsellor trust herself and her abilities and training, that she trusts also in the process of the counselling work, and that of the client's growing trust in herself.

Client's trust in me

My client needs to trust in me as a counsellor before any progress can be made in the work, and the establishment of this is slow and in direct proportion to how damaged the client's basic trust has been in previous encounters and relationships. A person who has been very deeply betrayed will be understandably slow to trust again. It is hoped that the particular relationship described earlier, built upon the core conditions, will be strong enough and convincing enough for my client to risk exploration of known and unknown depths of her being. This concentrated listening and unconditional acceptance may for a while unnerve some clients, who may never before have encountered this kind of relationship. Unexpected and different, the eventual result is often a growing trust in the counsellor, who is experienced and 'knows what she is doing'. At the beginning this trust can be total, with the client investing the counsellor with expertise and power, which the counsellor is anxious to return to the client. The counsellor cannot prevent the client from offering this control, but refuses to adopt a power stance. She tries to illustrate her trust in the client as 'expert' on herself. It is when the client begins to recognise and accept that she cannot shift responsibility or decision-making on to the person of the counsellor, that she hopefully and tentatively begins to trust herself. This can be a very difficult transition point. When clients appear to look to me for direction or advice, I do not always verbally refuse to give it, yet neither do I take on the role of expert, but like Rogers, 'I simply do not *behave* as an authority figure.'[3]

I remember a client of mine, when facing an impasse in our work, where he appeared to be completely stuck, said: 'Well, at least I know that you have a plan, and know where we're going, so I guess it will be eventually OK.' He was very upset when I told him that, on the contrary, I did not have a plan or direction for him to follow: 'I do get the sense that you're waiting for me to reveal the solution to this, so I feel it only fair to tell you that I don't. I couldn't possibly know what is best for you, but I do believe that somewhere *you* have the answer and I'm willing to help you to find it'. For some sessions he was terrified and anxious and angry at me, and then he gradually began to accept that it was frightening, but also in some ways exciting, to begin to make his own choices and decisions, which he had never had to do before, especially when he was not alone in his exploration.

Clients also need to trust in my ability to hear and to survive their story, and to learn, if slowly, that what I say, I will do and what I contract, I will deliver. We earn trust by fulfilling our promises, by proving that we are trustworthy, and perhaps even by succeeding in the tests our clients sometimes prepare for us. For example, I have known clients who are very loth to end a session and leave, holding the door while still talking. Assuming I have contracted for one hour, it is important that I hold to the hour, because herein is safety for the client. She needs to know that her time will not stretch and expand, or shrink, and will not depend on the material presented or whether she arrived late for the session. In order to foster this trust, I will respect my client's confidentiality, I will believe her story, I will allow her to set the pace, I will be patient, until she chooses to entrust her long-hidden secrets to me.

Trust in my client
I need to trust and to respect my client's perceptions and findings concerning herself, because she is the authority on herself in a way that I can never be. 'The approach is trust-centered rather than problem-centered.'[4] Clients who appear to

have given up, to be hopeless and helpless and suicidal, often uncover some tiny sign of hope on which they can begin to build a future. When I see nothingness, they can glimpse a potential, a possibility. And it is this repeated experience that sustains me with the most desperate of clients, and enables me to sit in the midst of uncertainty, without plan or map or direction. A client who spoke often of suicide surprised me when she said:

> I find myself in the pit of despair and I wish it were all over. And then I tell myself that this is no time to make important decisions about my life, or my death, and that I will wait until I am on my way up and out, and then I'll decide to end it all. Then of course I feel better and don't do it.

This continued to work for her during the course of our relationship! This trust in the 'constructive directional flow of the human being towards a more complex and complete development' is the basic element in the PCA: 'if I trust the capacity of the human individual for developing her own potentiality, then I can … permit her to choose her own way and her own direction.'[5]

I have worked with clients who struggle to correctly identify what it is they are feeling in a precise moment, as feelings shade into and mask each other. They are trying accurately to relate to this part of themselves so that they can use their knowledge as a stepping-stone to their next stage of self-knowledge. My client will not be well served if I hazard guesses and or merely offer different words or phrases, because I can ultimately trust my client to *know* if a word or description matches her inner self.

Client: I can't describe it. It's like being angry, but I'm not angry with her.

Me: Anger is close but not quite accurate?

Client: In some ways I'm sorry for her, but I don't want to be sorry for her. That hurts too much because I so want her to be happy.

Me: So you're hurt if you allow yourself to see her unhappiness.

Client: It's easier if I tell myself that she could be happy if she tried and she's not trying. (And she wept.)

Me: Her unhappiness really gets to you.

Client: (Through tears) I am angry with her because she hurts me, and I always thought I could love her into being happy. If I'm angry at her then her misery doesn't hurt me so much.

My client was relieved because she could now understand her chaotic feelings, which I could not have unravelled for her. If she had merely identified the anger, the hurt would have remained hidden and therefore unchangeable. Her hurt is so great and so painful that anger takes its place as a more manageable emotion. She had cast around until she found the accurate match, identifying descriptive word with feeling, and no half-correct identification would have succeeded in this clarification.

If a client is exploring her unhappiness, but not able to connect with or remember its cause, what I may experience in the session is an underlying feeling of misery, apparently disconnected and floating. My client may not be able to share coherently, from her place of felt distress, but may be shaken with fear and unhappiness, without words to explain. She cannot say what it is she needs to work with, because she has not as yet processed this material, so she presents her feelings around it. My task may be to try and be a non-anxious presence in the midst of the client's anxiety. It is important that I try to stay in this un-rational place, with the unattached fear, in the hope that she will eventually source the pain and seek her own solution.

Jacqueline Spring wrote of her experience of her counsellor *allowing* her to live her own life and go her own way. 'What she was telling me was I would, I could look after myself. She at any rate trusted my ability to do so, even when I did not... What she was offering was her faith in my ability to make it.' And this proved to be a major turning point in her therapy.[6] It is difficult at times for me to remember that I only see my client for one hour in her week, and only in the context of our sessions. And at times clients make such great strides and changes between sessions, that we can wonder at their need to come at all!

Trusting in the process

I try also to remember to trust in the *process* of counselling. At times clients can experience great relief at having actually decided to come for counselling, and having managed to articulate much stored stress and unhappiness. But of course just telling about it doesn't take it away. The next step in their work can be an unexpected increase in their pain as they dip below the surface and begin truly to explore their inner selves. I often

hear clients say angrily: 'What is happening? Why have I started this? I feel much worse than I did when I began', and some
people go away at this point. I find this distressing as I believe
that if they stay with the pain and the difficulty, they will begin
to understand their selves and come to find resolutions. The
process does work, but I do fear for those who opt out too
early. Thankfully the majority of clients continue.

When my client appears to be totally stuck, or when I am
sitting with a deeply depressed person who is asking 'what is
the point?' and there does not appear to be any, then I can
remind myself to trust in my beliefs about the nature of the
work, and so far this has never failed me. The process continues
to unfold and my client shifts, often in a totally unexpected
direction and after a considerable length of time! These beliefs
have been telescoped into a set of propositions by Bozarth and
Temaner Brodley which are further summarised here.[7]

The person-centred counsellor believes that every individual
has internal resources for growth, and that when a counsellor
offers the core conditions of congruence, empathy and acceptance, therapeutic movement is likely to occur. She believes further that human nature is essentially constructive and social,
motivated to seek the truth, and that self-regard is a basic
human need. She holds that a person's perceptions determine
their experience and behaviour, and that individuals should be
related to as whole and developing persons. Individuals should
be the primary reference point in any helping activities; and
they should be treated as doing their best to grow and preserve
themselves. It is essential that the counsellor reject the pursuit
of authority or power in the relationship, and instead actively
seek to share power. 'A counsellor who feels unable to subscribe
to these propositions is unlikely to be able to practise person-
centred counselling as we understand the term in this book.'[8]

It would be very difficult to work within a system about which we had basic doubts. Of course in times of stress and uncertainty, even the most dedicated PCA practitioner will experience doubts, but overall belief in the process is essential if we are to work effectively within it. This is more possible the more experienced we are, because if we have seen these beliefs proving effective so often, then we can lean more confidently on our theoretical base. At the beginning of our training, we are asked to put our own trust in tutors and writers, and it is only when we can take the risk of 'trusting the process' that we can see for ourselves the tangible results that follow.

And paradoxically this trust in the process goes hand in hand with the central uncertianty of counselling. 'The capacity to tolerate uncertainty is a prerequisite for the profession... therapists frequently wobble, improvise, and grope for direction.'[9] We, both my client and myself, search for certainty and meaning in a world that so often has neither, and we are forced instead to try and cope with what Yalom calls the 'givens' of existence. These are the inevitability of death for ourselves and those we love; the freedom to make our lives as we will and the weight of responsibility this brings; our ultimate aloneness; the absence of obvious meaning to life. He further describes therapy as 'a caring, deeply human meeting between two people, one (generally, but not always, the patient) more troubled than the other',[10] which carries echoes of Casement: 'in every consulting room there ought to be two rather frightened people: the patient and the psychoanalyst.'[11]

Working within the client/counsellor relationship, we constantly try to listen to the music rather than focus solely on the dance, trying to move beyond the practicalities to the mood, the tension, the energy between us. It is in the letting go of effort that we find the link and the connection where we can give each other permission to be weak and vulnerable, and courage to seek out change and new strengths. Hawkins suggests that it is in this space *between* counsellor and client, that change may happen.[12] This is a transformative space, where if we give up trying and just *allow* ourselves to be, in the relationship, something new emerges without specific plan or shape, a moment of faith in the process, where we have created, or more accurately, allowed 'space for grace' thus allowing movement, rather than trying to force it. The texture of what we say is of greater importance than the words we use.

Trusting in myself as counsellor

I need also to trust in myself, to be in contact with my own deeper feeling levels. 'I *trust* the feelings, words, impulses, fantasies that emerge in me. In this way I am using more than my conscious self, drawing on some of the capacities of my whole organism.'[13] It is not easy for the counsellor at the beginning of her career to trust sufficiently in herself. Books and tutors appear to have a much greater ability to be wise, to know exactly what to say. Yet being congruent means being in contact with our inner selves, and being willing to share this knowledge. Whether our words and our sharing are honed or pretty, they are *real* and they come from our inner selves, and this is what engenders real trust, not clever ideas or phrases. This trust will also be based on my belief that I will do my best in this situation, and that I can do no more than my best, whatever my training or my experience. Perfection has no place in the counselling room, from either counsellor or client. If I am genuinely trying to offer the core conditions to my client, and retaining my focus on her, then I can trust in myself in that moment. There will always be those who could do differently, or more effectively, but I am the person who is here, right now, with this client.

Becoming an accredited counsellor is never a point of finally arriving, but rather a new beginning, and membership of a professional association ensures ongoing learning, constant supervision, and adherence to a code of ethical practice. Trusting in myself as counsellor never means becoming complacent about my 'skills' or 'relationship techniques'. It does mean accepting myself as a good-enough counsellor, as being as good a counsellor as I can be in this moment, as being willing to try and stay with and accept my client. 'I needed someone who was so *secure* in themselves that they could reach out to *me*.'[14] We need also to remain aware of the difficulty of this work, and the demands it makes on us. I sometimes have an image of a reservoir from which people make constant 'withdrawals', and if it is not regularly replenished it will eventually run dry and have nothing more to give. I need to nourish my inner life, and my basic self, lest I find myself one day unable to be the counsellor I would like to be. Every time I travel by plane, I am reminded of this when the flight attendants tell us that, in the case of emergency, if we are travelling with children, we attend to our own oxygen masks first and *then* help the child. It can sound unnatural, but it makes practical sense.

It is important too that the counsellor retain her sense of self, her integrity, and this can take the form of sharing with the client the impact of her statements or criticisms on us. A student who worked with a most intrusive client found that this was impeding the work. Her client loitered outside the building where they worked, watched her to her car, and consistently asked questions about her family, where she shopped, what books she read, and generally focused more on her curiosity about the counsellor than on her own work. After some weeks, the counsellor shared her dislike of the invasive questions and explained that she was not comfortable with the focus outside the sessions. Quite aggressively the client retorted that 'This is not all about you, you know', and the counsellor replied: 'I do know that, but this is a relationship and I am part of it.' The client responded positively to the counsellor's honest and straightforward approach, and the work progressed to where the client was able to own and focus on her role in her other relationships outside counselling which was quite controlling and where she needed to be always 'better' than the other person.

Rogers wrote of his relationship with his clients: 'What I wish is to be at her side, occasionally falling a step behind, occasionally a step ahead when I see more clearly the path we are on, and only taking a leap when guided by my intuition.'[15] I can wish for no more!

The client's trust in herself

As we saw earlier, a client's locus of approval may be firmly placed outside of herself. She believes that others know better than she does what is good for her, and she is fearful of making decisions which bring responsibility for the outcome. It is hoped that counselling will enable her to become a fully-functioning person, capable of trusting in her own self, in her plans, and in her ability to organise and live her life according to her own set of values. It is quite marvellous to see a fearful, indecisive and unhappy person slowly (so slowly) become confident, less fearful and more contented in herself. She has become able to trust in herself, in her intuition, to look at her previous experience and extract the lessons which will be helpful to her today, to be more fully herself in her relationships. And of course this is the reward for us as counsellors, to allow ourselves to acknowledge that we played a part in this change. The client did the work and the changing, but we created the safe space within which she could do so. It can be difficult for students and trainee counsellors to acknowledge their part in this process, and at times difficult also for experienced counsellors to do so. But if we do not acknowledge our due credit, and allow ourselves 'job satisfaction', why would we continue to work as counsellors? If I do not believe, and acknowledge to myself, the effective pieces of my work, then who else will praise and encourage me? To say to myself 'well done' and perhaps even to mark or reward a particularly difficult session can be important if I am to take pride in myself as counsellor.

It is sometimes asked why counsellors do the work they do, so difficult and demanding, often not recognised, and not always ending as we might wish. If we did not get some benefit or reward, if the work were not in same way 'growth-promoting' for me as counsellor, could I listen day after day to the unhappiness and despair? Surely there are less wearing ways of earning my living. Brazier postulated a further need in the human person, a need 'to regard others positively', a need not only to be loved, but also to love others. If this 'intrinsic altruism'[16] is not accepted by another person, or if we do not have an outlet for it, then he suggested that the impact is as severe as when we do not receive love for ourselves. If he is correct, then this may be why I work as a counsellor, and it also helps in understanding the sadness of some of my clients.

Transferred feelings
As this is one of the areas of greatest difference between PCA and other theories, I will mention it briefly from the PCA point of view. Rogers believed that the emotions and feelings of clients towards their therapists fell into two categories. Firstly there were the feelings of, for example, resentment towards a counsellor who has unwittingly responded inappropriately

towards the client, or assumed a mantle of superiority, or given unwelcome instructions. The resentment is the direct result of something this counsellor has done or said. These feelings can also be positive, as where a client may be grateful for 'small actions showing concern for the client's comfort'[17] such as checking if a fire is too hot, offering a glass of water for a persistent cough, expressing sympathy for a bereavement.

The second category are the client's feelings towards the counsellor which have little to do with the counsellor's behaviour, but spring from within the client and are projected on to the person of the counsellor. These may also be positive or negative, and are unconsciously transferred from their real origin (parents, part of the client's self) to the counsellor. The client is identifying the counsellor with significant persons in his life and is reacting accordingly in line with how he reacted to these people in his past. These transferred feelings are inappropriate to the present relationship.

'From a client-centered point of view, it is not necessary, in responding to and dealing with these feelings, to determine whether they are therapist-caused or are projections. The distinction is of theoretical interest, but is not a practical problem.'[18] Rogers believed that the client will explore and openly discuss these negative or positive feelings, whether transferred from others or not, if the counsellor can be open and understanding and acceptant of them. This acceptance enables the client to recognise that these feelings are hers, within herself. The counsellor will work with the awareness, and the emerging awareness of the client, and will not 'wander' into the unconscious. It is not, therefore, that PCA denies this transfer of feelings, but it has a different way of looking at them and a different way of acknowledging and working with them. It maintains that we work with the feelings of the client, openly and honestly, rather than at all times with 'the transference'. 'To deal with transference feelings as a very special part of therapy, making their handling the very core of therapy, is to my mind a grave mistake.' [19]

Of course Rogers acknowledged the unconscious, but he did not focus his work there. By definition, the unconscious is not yet 'known' to the client, and therefore the client cannot be 'expert' in its contents, cannot 'know' what it holds. As person-centred counselling maintains that 'the client knows where it hurts', then it will not work in this as yet 'unknown' area. Mearns and Thorne go further when they write about working with the unconscious: 'Perhaps this is what makes it so attractive to therapists – it allows the therapist unbridled power to exercise theory and imagination without possibility of contradiction.' [20]

Such inappropriate transfer of feelings may also occur within the counsellor, who can at times react unconsciously to the client as she did in earlier relationships. I remember a twenty-one-year-old client who was too thin, dressed always in black, and who spoke almost in a whisper, and curled up in her chair as she spoke to me. I fretted and worried unduly about her, ached within whenever she came, and at times came close to offering her a bowl of soup! It was my supervisor who eventually jolted my memory of a very similar person, a friend of mine who had taken her own life some years before. I realised that I was identifying and reaching out to this girl, as I had unsuccessfully tried to reach my now dead friend. In so doing, I was losing sight of my client's individuality and not focusing on her unique person and problems. It was a salutary lesson.

PCA and me

It surprises me to look back and see how my personal life has been so inextricably linked with my life as a working counsellor. Perhaps this is an illustration of what Carl Rogers described

a 'a way of being', that the PCA has comprehensively trans-
formed my way of living. The advantages are obvious to me
when I am aware, for example, of being able not to interrupt at
the beginning of a story which needs to be shared, when I am
able not to respond angrily to a friend's heedless or critical
remark, when I am able to highlight the feeling of loss or fear
beneath a tedious complaint. These far outweigh the disadvan-
tages, as when I find myself listening too closely and too
intensely to chatter at a party, or when I sense sadness beneath
a casual statement, but am aware that acknowledgement of this
would be intrusive in the circumstances. Having learned to listen in a special way can often mean that we hear more than we
would like!

Counselling is much more accepted today than when I started, and is taking its place among the professions. This brings its
own responsibilities: 'Ultimately counselling and therapies that
patch people up and leave them in the same, continuously damaging society, are a waste of energy',[21] but this call to action is
rarely followed.

At this time proposals for statutory regulation for counsellors and psychotherapists are at an advanced stage and this is a
positive step towards regulating our diverse field. It is an effort
to ensure that all those who work in this area have basic training, adhere to basic principles and standards, and are fully
accountable. It is to be hoped, however, that our professional
destiny will not be dictated as a result by law makers, and that
our 'best-practice' policies will not be driven by insurance con-
siderations.

Counselling and psychotherapy may be a young profession,
but it has made great strides in the mental health field in this
short time. It has been said that counsellors are not – by the
very nature of their work – activists or revolutionaries or lob-

byists, but Carl Rogers was none of these and yet his 'revolution' has been far-reaching and influential. Perhaps we counsellors can borrow from his example. Looking at the future of counselling prompts the remark: 'A lot done – more to do'. I feel I have contributed to the growth of counselling in Ireland, and also that I have fulfilled the earlier dreams of our small study group of the fifties. Counselling and I have worked well together.

Notes

1. Jerold D. Bozarth *Person-Centered Therapy: A Revolutionary Paradigm,* (PCCS Books UK, 1998) 117.
2. Carl Rogers 'A Client-Centered, Person-Centered Approach to Therapy' in *Psychotherapist's Casebook: Theory and Technique in Practice,* eds. I.L. Kutash and A. Wolf (Jossey-Bass USA, 1986) 3.
3. *The Carl Rogers Reader* eds. Howard Kirschenbaum and Valerie Land Henderson, (Constable London, 1990) 141.
4. Bozarth, *Person-Centered Therapy* 116.
5. *The Carl Rogers Reader* 313.
6. Jacqueline Spring *Cry Hard and Swim* (Virago Press London, 1987) 75.
7. Bozarth, J. and Temaner Brodley, B. 'The Core Values and Theory of the Person-Centered Approach: Paper prepared for the First Annual Meeting of the Association for the Development of the Person-Centered Approach', Chicago 1986: quoted in *Person-Centred Counselling in Action* by Dave Mearns and Brian Thorne 20.
8. *Person-Centred Counselling in Action* Dave Mearns and Brian Thorne Sage 1999 19.
9. Irvin D. Yalom *Love's Executioner* (Penguin, 1991) 13.
10. Ibid., 13.
11. Patrick Casement *On Learning from the Patient* (London: Routledge, 1985).
12. P. Hawkins during talk to AGM of Irish Association for Counselling and Psychotherapy, Dublin, 27 March 2004.
13. Carl Rogers 'On Encounter Groups' (1970) quoted in D. Brazier, ed., *Beyond Carl Rogers,* (Constable, London, 1993) 27.
14. David Howe *On Being a Client* (Sage, London, 1993) 37.

15. Carl Rogers 'A Client-Centered, Person-Centered Approach to Therapy' in *Psychotherapist's Casebook: Theory and Technique in Practice* eds. I.L. Kutash and A. Wolf (Jossey-Bass USA, 1986) 25.
16. *Beyond Carl Rogers* 78.
17. *The Carl Rogers Reader* 129.
18. Ibid., 130.
19. Ibid., 134.
20. *Person-Centred Therapy Today* 176.
21. Colin Feltham in letter to *Counselling: The Journal of the British Association for Counselling* No. 61 1987 36.

Appendix

What is counselling/psychotherapy?
It is generally accepted that counselling/psychotherapy has the potential to change people's lives. The overall aim is to facilitate a focused exploration of particular concerns, in order that people may live in more satisfying and resourceful ways as individuals and as members of the broader society.

Counselling/psychotherapy also helps people to identify how they would realistically like their lives to be, and how they could make decisions and embrace change.

It also aims to help clients explore difficulties of a more precise nature, such as troubled marriages, addiction, bereavement, social phobias, and so on.

Definitions.
1.
The overall aim of counselling and psychotherapy is to provide the client with opportunities to explore, discover and clarify ways of living that are more satisfying and resourceful. Counselling and psychotherapy incorporate the giving of time, attention and respect in a confidential relationship. This includes work with individuals, pairs or groups of people referred to as 'clients'.

The counsellor/psychotherapist's role is to facilitate the client's growth in ways that respect the person's values, personal resources and capacity for self determination. Only when both parties explicitly agree to enter into a counselling relationship, and a contract is agreed between the counsellor/psychotherapist and client, does it become counselling/psychotherapy.

Regardless of the theoretical approaches preferred by individual counsellors, there are ethical issues which are common to all counselling situations.
(Irish Association for Counselling/Psychotherapy, 2003)

2.
Counselling involves a deliberately undertaken contract with clearly agreed boundaries and commitment to privacy and confidentiality. It requires explicit and informed agreement. The counsellor's role is to facilitate the client's work in ways which respect the client's values, personal resources and capacity for choice within his or her cultural context.
(British Association for Counselling and Psychotherapy, 1998)

3.
Counselling is an interactive learning process contracted between counsellor(s) and client(s), be they individuals, families, groups or institutions, which approaches in a holistic way, social, cultural, economic and/or emotional issues.

Counselling may be concerned with addressing and resolving specific problems, making decisions, coping with crisis, improving relationships, developmental issues, promoting and developing personal awareness, working with feelings, thoughts, perceptions and internal or external con-

flict. The overall aim is to provide clients with opportunities to work in self-defined ways, towards living in more satisfying and resourceful ways as individuals and as members of the broader society.
(European Association for Counselling, 1995)

How does counselling/psychotherapy work?
Counselling/psychotherapy takes place within a specific kind of interpersonal relationship, which is neither informal nor spontaneous, but rather a deliberately undertaken contract with clearly and mutually agreed boundaries. Research shows that this relationship between counsellor/psychotherapist and client is the most important factor in a successful outcome. The focus throughout is on the client's needs and problems, and the work may be long or short-term, depending on the nature of the difficulties presented by the client, and the theoretical orientation of the counsellor/psychotherapist.

This therapeutic alliance will constitute a safe space within which the client feels free to discuss all aspects of him or herself, without fear of judgement or censure, or misuse of power on the part of the counsellor/psychotherapist. The boundaries will encompass ethical and professional imperatives, as well as confidentiality, secure settings, time-keeping and appointment times.

The counsellor/psychotherapist
The creation and maintenance of such a relationship imposes a heavy demand on the counsellor/psychotherapist. Obviously communication and listening skills are essential, but more important is the counsellor/psychotherapist's ability to sustain and foster trust in the relationship and in the process, and also the ability to tolerate the high level of stress and uncertainty reflected by the client.

He or she will accept clients as they are, with respect for their values and beliefs, will not judge nor criticise them, and will be open and honest about his or her part in the relationship.

A high standard of training is essential for a counsellor/psychotherapist to fulfill these requirements, and the nature and length of training is a current topic for debate. It is further required of the counsellor/psychotherapist that he/she sustain a constant self-monitoring and on-going professional development, and lifelong supervision of the work is a requirement for most accreditation schemes.

Bibliography

Barrett-Lennard, Godfrey T. *Carl Rogers' Helping System: Journey and Substance* (Sage, 1998)

Belton, Neil *The Good Listener* (Weidenfeld and Nicholson, 1998)

Berman, Linda *Beyond the Smile: The Therapeutic Use of the Photograph* (Routledge, 1993)

Bettelheim, Bruno *Freud and Man's Soul* (Flamingo, 1985)

Boyne, Edward *Psychotherapy in Ireland* (Columba, 1993)

Bozarth, Jerold D., and Brodley, B.T., 'The Core Values and Theory of the Person-Centered Approach'. (A paper presented at the first annual meeting of the Association for the Development of the Person-Centered Approach) International House, Chicago, USA, 1986.

Bozarth, Jerold D. *Person-Centered Therapy: A Revolutionary Paradigm* (PCCS Books, 1998)

Brazier, David *Beyond Carl Rogers* (Constable, 1993)

Brazier, David *Zen Therapy* (Constable, 1995)

Carroll, Lewis *Through the Looking Glass* (1872) (The Bodley Head, 1974)

Cohen, David *Carl Rogers – A Critical Biography* (Constable, 1997)

Hawkins, P. and Shohet, R. *Supervision in the Helping Professions*

(Milton Keynes, Open University Press, 1989)

Halmos, Paul *The Faith of the Counsellors* (Constable, 1981)

Howe, David *On Being a Client* (Sage, 1993)

Hubble, Mark A., Duncan, Barry L., Miller, Scott D., eds., *The Heart and Soul of Change* (American Psychological Association, 1999)

Jones, Phil *Drama as Therapy. Theatre as Living* (Routledge, 1995)

Kirschenbaum, Howard and Land Henderson, Valerie, eds., *The Carl Rogers Reader* (Constable, 1990)

Kutash, I.L. and Wolf, A. eds., 'A Client-centered/Person-centered Approach to Therapy' in *Psychotherapist's Casebook: Theory and Technique in Practice* (Jossey-Bass Inc., 1986)

Spring, Jacqueline *Cry Hard and Swim* (Virago Press, 1987)

Lendrum, Susan and Syme, Gabrielle *Gift of Tears* (Routledge, 1992)

Levant, R. and Shlien, J., eds., *Client Centered Therapy and the Person-Centered Approach* (Praeger, 1984)

Maslow, A. *Towards a Psychology of Being* (Van Nostrand, 1968)

Mearns, Dave and Thorne, Brian *Person-Centred Counselling in Action* (Sage, 1999)

Mearns, Dave and Thorne Brian *Person-Centred Therapy Today* (Sage, 2000)

Mearns, Dave *Developing Person-Centred Counselling* (Sage, 1994)

Mearns, Dave *Person-Centred Counselling Training* (Sage, 1997)

Merry Tony *Invitation to Person-Centred Psychology* (Whurr, 1997)

Milner Pat and Palmer Stephen, eds., *The BACP Counselling Reader Vol. 2* (Sage, in association with BACP, 2001)

Nightingale, Constance *Journey of a Survivor and other Poems* (Self-published, 1986)

O'Farrell, Ursula *Courage to Change* (Veritas, 1999)

O'Farrell, Ursula *First Steps in Counselling* (Veritas, 1988)

Orbach, Susie *The Impossibility of Sex* (Penguin, 1999)

Palmer, Stephen and Ved, Varma, eds., *The Future of Counselling and Psychotherapy* (Sage, 1997)

Phillips, Adam *Promises, Promises* (Faber and Faber, 2000)

Rogers, Carl and Dymond, R.F,. eds. *Psychotherapy and Personality Change* (University of Chicago Press) (Article: case of Mrs. Oak)

Rogers, Carl and Sanford, Ruth C. 'Client-Centered Psychotherapy' in *Comprehensive Textbook of Psychiatry, IV* Kaplan, H.I. and Sadock, B.J., eds., (Williams & Wilkins, 1984)

Rogers, Carl 'A Client-Centered, Person-Centered Approach to Therapy' in *Psychotherapist's Casebook: Theory and Technique in Practice* Kutash, I.L. and Wolf, A. eds., (Jossey-Bass, 1986)

Rogers, Carl *A Way of Being* (Houghton Mifflin, 1980)

Rogers, Carl *Freedom to Learn for the 80s* (Charles E. Merrill Publications, 1983)

Thorne, Brian and Lambers Elke, eds., *Person-Centred Therapy – A European Perspective* (Sage, 1998)

Thorne, Brian *Carl Rogers* (Sage, 1992)

Thorne, Brian *Person-Centred Counselling* (Whurr, 1991)

Van Belle, H.A. *Basic Intent and Therapeutic Approach of Carl R. Rogers* (Wedge Publishing, 1980)

Wilkins, Paul *Person-Centred Therapy in Focus* (Sage, 2003)

Yalom, Irvin D. *Love's Executioner* (Penguin, 1991)

Yalom, Irvin D. *The Gift of Therapy* (Piatkus, 2002)

Publications

Eisteach: A Quarterly Journal of Counselling and Psychotherapy Published by Irish Assoc. for Counselling and Psychotherapy Vol. 2 Nos. 8, 11, 25 1999 and 2003

Index